Maya® 6
KillerTips

M A Y A 6 KILLER TIPS

Maya 6 Killer Tips Team

EDITOR
Karyn Johnson

PRODUCTION EDITOR
Connie Jeung-Mills

CONTRIBUTORS
Erick Miller
Eric Pender

TECHNICAL EDITORS
Greg Berridge
Adrian Dimond

COPY EDITOR
Nancy Reinhardt

PROOFREADER
Haig MacGregor

INDEXER
Rebecca Plunkett

COVER DESIGN AND CREATIVE CONCEPTS
Felix Nelson

COVER PRODUCTION
Aren Howell

COMPOSITOR
Owen Wolfson

Published by New Riders Publishing / Peachpit Press

Copyright © 2005 by New Riders Publishing

First edition: August 2004

Composed in Myriad and Helvetica.

Trademarks
All terms mentioned in this book that are known to be trademarks or service marks have been appropriately capitalized. New Riders Publishing / Peachpit Press cannot attest to the accuracy of this information. Use of a term in the book should not be regarded as affecting the validity of any trademark or service mark. Maya is a registered trademark of Alias, Inc.; Windows is a registered trademark of Microsoft Corporation in the United States and/or other countries.

Warning and Disclaimer
This book is designed to provide information about Maya 6 tips. Every effort has been made to make this book as complete and as accurate as possible, but no warranty of fitness is implied.

The information is provided on an as-is basis. The authors and New Riders Publishing / Peachpit Press shall have neither liability nor responsibility to any person or entity with respect to any loss or damages arising from the information contained in this book or from the use of the discs or programs that may accompany it.

ISBN 0-321-27853-4

9 8 7 6 5 4 3 2

Printed and bound in the United States of America

www.peachpit.com
www.scottkelbybooks.com

To the three girls, source of all things good in my world.

—ERIC HANSON

To my mom, who inspires and supports me in all I do; my dad, for his love;

and my brother Steve, who makes me proud.

—KENNETH IBRAHIM

To my wonderful wife and son, who bring nothing but happiness into my life.

—ALEX NIJMEH

Eric Hanson is a visual effects artist specializing in digital environments and effects for feature films. Originally an architect, he established early 3D visualization studios for some of the country's largest architectural firms, including The Callison Partnership, in Seattle and Gensler, in Los Angeles. An expanding interest in film led to a move into visual effects work, resulting in senior CG artist positions with leading visual effects houses Digital Domain, Sony Imageworks, Dream Quest Images, Walt Disney Feature Animation, and SimEx Digital Studios. His work can be seen in *Spider-Man, Cast Away, Hollow Man, Mission to Mars, Bicentennial Man, Fantasia 2000, Atlantis,* and *The Fifth Element,* as well as many large-format, special-venue films worldwide.

Eric specializes in 3D work with Maya, RenderMan, and Shake, and is an active teacher of those packages. He has taught for several years, having instructed courses on advanced 3D techniques at SGI's Silicon Studio and Gnomon School of Visual Effects, and is currently leading a curriculum on visual effects at the University of Southern California's School of Cinema-TV. He frequently speaks and holds workshops at various trade shows and schools domestically, as well as in Japan, even though he is not sure what to eat while there.

Eric is a member of ACM/Siggraph and the Visual Effects Society and holds a professional degree in Architecture from the University of Texas at Austin.

Eric can be reached at his web site, **www.visuraimaging.com**.

ABOUT THE AUTHORS

Kenneth Ibrahim began his career in visual effects as an Alias|Wavefront application engineer in Tokyo, Japan in 1994, just as Maya was entering its alpha phase. After returning to the U.S. and spending a total of three years at A|W demonstrating and supporting Maya, Ken moved into production proper by joining PDI's C.A.F.E. group and working on a number of TV spots during which he helped integrate Maya into the PDI pipeline. Ken has since worked at a number of production companies on such films as *Shrek, Final Fantasy, Matrix Revolutions, X2, Peter Pan*, and *I, Robot*. He has focused on FX animation/development and lighting and spends a good deal of time MEL-scripting and API coding. Ken graduated from Santa Clara University with a degree in computer engineering before moving to Japan with the goal of becoming fluent in Japanese. While there, he taught English, programmed Macintosh computers, and went to work for SEGA, writing software tools and creating graphics in the AM3 R&D department. His voice was also featured in a number of arcade games including the hit *SEGA Rally Championship* and *Virtua Cop*. When not at the office, he likes to keep busy with various hobbies including music composition and recording, language study, reading, working out, and traveling. He recently spent two months studying Italian in Rome and is preparing another trip somewhere after his current project is complete. Ken has also recently published a Japanese vocabulary building book based on words he learned watching the Japanese anime *Akira*. Ken has created a number of items that are available at *shop.shuri-ken.com*. He can be reached at his Web site *www.shuri-ken.com*.

Alex Nijmeh is currently a digital artist at Digital Domain, based in Los Angeles, CA. Specializing in 3D modeling and lighting, Alex recently finished working on Roland Emmerich's blockbuster film *The Day After Tomorrow*, where he contributed to the ambitious effort to digitally model a large portion of NYC, and moved on to his next feature film *I, Robot*. Even before working in visual effects, Alex has been a long time Maya user, since version 2.0. He worked for several years as Lead Modeler and Senior Designer at a San Francisco–based company that produced immersive film-like quality environments and cinematics for a unique virtual reality venue. He has also used Maya to produce work for television commercials, a TV pilot for a police drama series, as well as illustrations for PC games and professional software packages. Alex grew up and attended school in San Jose, California and has a BFA in computer graphics. Alex can be reached via email at *alex3d1@comcast.net*.

Erick Miller is currently a lead technical director at Digital Domain, the Academy Award–winning visual effects company responsible for digital effects in recent block-busters such as *I, Robot, The Day After Tomorrow, Lord of the Rings,* and *X-Men.* Since Erick has been at DD, he has contributed to many projects: a plug-in pose-based eformation system, a proprietary muscle/skin deformation plug-in system, and a crowd animation and rendering system, just to name a few. After wrapping up on the Maya-based facial rigging for a photo-realistic CG that Michael Jordan used in Gatorade's 2002 Super Bowl commercial, Erick created a Maya-based crowd pipeline for Roland Emmerich's apocalyptic end-of-the-world feature film *The Day After Tomorrow.* After that, Erick moved on to build a Character TD team for the feature film, *I, Robot.* As a lead technical director, Erick was responsible for the hero facial rigging of the fully CG, photo-realistic main character, "Sonny," as well the character-based Maya pipeline, scripts, plug-ins, and character tools. Some of Erick's favorite duties include advanced character setup, facial rigging and complex skin deformations. Besides character setup, Erick also often enjoys connecting his creative knowledge with MEL scripting, Maya's API, and other external programming languages and C/C++ APIs to further advance a character-based pipeline. Erick is a Maya Master Class presenter, has contributed to the authoring of two books on Maya (Inside Maya and Maya 5 Killer Tips), is Alias|Wavefront certified in Character Setup, has a Bachelor of Fine Arts degree in Computer Graphics from the Academy of Art College, and has been a Maya user since its inception at version 1.0.

Eric Pender has been creating 3D effects animation on feature films since 1996. He has worked on movies such as *Alien Resurrection, Batman and Robin, Hard Rain, Air Force One, Sphere, Gone in Sixty Seconds, Mission to Mars,* and *Kangaroo Jack,* as well as the opening sequence for *Wonderful World of Disney* on ABC. He started out working for Alias|Wavefront in Santa Barbara and specializing in Dynamation, which was the original dynamics package created by Wavefront. Dynamation was used as the frame-work for the dynamics package in Maya. Eric has been using Maya in production since the first version.

ACKNOWLEDGMENTS

Without rambling on endlessly like a weepy Oscar acceptance speech, I would like to briefly wish a warm thanks to many of those who laid the train tracks down in front of me or added coal to the engine along the way. First and foremost, much love must go to my beautiful wife Kari and our little love buckets, Taylor and Shelby. 3D artists often mistake the world as one big rendering, and Kari constantly keeps me in check by reminding me that it is indeed much more. She has endured my crazed and relentless obsession with CGI for many years with amazing tolerance and support. Kari, it has been noted by management and you are in line for a modest bonus soon!

Professionally, I have had many fellow adventurers on this train ride, but huge thanks go out to the truly supportive ones, like brother Bill Hanson of Apple Computer, FX animator extraordinaire Cody Harrington, and design maestro Joe Cordelle. I can attribute much of my success to their well-timed mutual prodding and encouragement. There have been numerous, enjoyable fellow travelers along the way, such as Mark Lefitz, Alex Nijmeh, Pat Finley, Chris Nichols, Travis Price, Ben Procter, Chris Cunningham, John Goodman, Allen Yamashita, and Eric Beggs, where it all started. Much has been learned (and laughed) from all.

Thanks go out to the quality team at New Riders and Peachpit, including Elise Walter and Karyn Johnson. I had four great contributors for this edition, Alex Nijmeh, Kenneth Ibrahim, Erick Miller, and Eric Pender. Thanks to my two eagle-eyed tech editors, Greg Berridge and Adrian Dimond. Lastly, great thanks go out to Scott Kelby for the Killer Idea of the Killer Tips series- onwards and upwards!

Then there is the inevitable thanks and love going out to my parents, who got the train out of the station and continue to support my constantly unfolding path while moving down the tracks.

—Eric Hanson

I would like to start by saying that none of this would have been possible for me without the loving support of my beautiful wife Susan and our adorable son Tyler, who believed in me and stood by my every decision. Susan, I can't even begin to describe my appreciation for you. I can't imagine where I would be now if it weren't for my good friend Eric Hanson who helped grease the wheels for me, and helped to get me where I am today with my career. A special thanks to my coworkers at Digital Domain who help make each day enjoyable. Pavel Prane, John Decker, Esdras Varagnolo, Ryan Vance, Andy Wilkoff, Paul George, Daniel Fazel, Patrick Finley, Melanie Okamura, Chris Nichols, Kevin Jackson, Dan Fowler, and I can't forget Charles Abou Aad, who endures the brunt of my sense of humor as he sits beside me, and who really suffers the most. Thanks, Charles, and great big thanks to my loving parents for always encouraging me to follow my dreams and to never settle for second best. A big thanks goes out to my brother Gabriel, and my Sister Elena, for their continued encouragement.

—Alex Nijmeh

ABOUT THE TECHNICAL REVIEWERS

These reviewers contributed their considerable hands-on expertise to the entire development process for *Maya 6 Killer Tips*. As the book was being written, these dedicated professionals reviewed all the material for technical content, organization, and flow. Their feedback was critical to ensuring that *Maya 6 Killer Tips* fits our readers' need for the highest-quality technical information.

Greg Berridge is currently the head instructor of the Digital Character Animation program at Vancouver Film School. He is a certified Maya Instructor holding accreditation in several areas of Maya expertise. Greg has completed work for several local Vancouver companies, including Lorax International. He has also spent time teaching Maya to content creators at Mainframe Entertainment. Greg has completed work for the NIAC (NASA Institute for Advanced Concepts) on the international front. First and foremost an instructor, Greg has been teaching Maya since it arrived six years ago. In addition to his professional endeavors, Greg is also working as an independent producer and is currently developing several concepts for television and film. He is also an aspiring author, hoping to have his own book published soon on the intricacies of Maya. Above all else, he is engrossed in Maya and breathes 3D content creation at every possible moment.

Adrian Dimond, an animator and designer currently residing in Los Angeles, works on a wide range of projects spanning the last decade. Recent projects include a flying bottle cap for Budweiser, visual effects for *Harold and Kumar go to White Castle* and a music video for an electroclash band called Lemans. Adrian shares his vast experience at *http://www.highend3d.com*, *http://www.cgtalk.com* and at his website *http://www.gmask.com/tutorials*

TABLE OF CONTENTS

TABLE OF CONTENTS

TABLE OF CONTENTS

TABLE OF CONTENTS

TABLE OF CONTENTS

TABLE OF CONTENTS

TABLE OF CONTENTS

Maya 6 Killer Tips
Edited by Scott Kelby

Welcome to *Maya 6 Killer Tips*. As Editor for the Killer Tips series, I can't tell you how excited and truly gratified I am to see this concept of creating a book that is cover-to-cover nothing but tips, extend from my original book (*Photoshop Killer Tips*) into *Maya 6 Killer Tips*.

The idea for this series of books came to me when I was at the bookstore looking through the latest Photoshop books on the shelf. I found myself doing the same thing to every book I picked up: I'd turn the page until I found a paragraph that started with the word "Tip." I'd read the tip, then I'd keep turning until I found another sidebar tip. I soon realized I was hooked on tips, because I knew that if I were writing the book that's where I'd put all my best material. Think about it: If you were writing a book, and you had a really cool tip, an amazing trick, or an inside secret or shortcut, you wouldn't bury it among hundreds of paragraphs of text. No way! You'd make it stand out: You'd put a box around it, maybe put a tint behind it, and if it was really cool (and short and sweet), you'd get everybody's attention by starting with the word "Tip!"

That's what got me thinking. Obviously, I'm not the only one who likes these tips, because almost every software book has them. There's only one problem: There's never *enough* of them. And I thought, "Wouldn't it be great if there were a book that was nothing but those cool little tips?" (Of course, the book wouldn't actually have sidebars, since what's in the sidebars would be the focus: nothing but cool shortcuts, inside secrets, slick ways to do the things we do everyday, but faster—and more fun— than ever!) That was the book I really wanted, and thanks to the wonderful people at New Riders, that's the book they let me write (along with my coauthor and good friend Felix Nelson). It was called *Photoshop Killer Tips*, and it became an instant bestseller because Felix and I were committed to creating something special: A book where every page included yet another tip that would make you nod your head, smile, and think "Ahhh, so that's how they do it."

TIP

If you were writing a book, and you had a really cool tip, an amazing trick, or an inside secret or shortcut, you wouldn't bury it among hundreds of paragraphs of text. You'd make it stand out: You'd put a box around it, maybe put a tint behind it, and if it was really cool (and short and sweet), you'd get everybody's attention by starting with the word "Tip!"

If you've ever wondered how the pros get twice the work done in half the time, it's really no secret: They do everything as efficiently as possible. They don't do *anything* the hard way. They know every timesaving shortcut, every workaround, every speed tip, and as such they work at full speed all the time. They'll tell you, when it comes to being efficient, and when it comes to staying ahead of the competition: Speed Kills!

Well, what you're holding in your hand is another Killer Tips book: A book packed cover-to-cover with nothing but those cool little sidebar tips (without the sidebars). Eric Hanson has captured the spirit and flavor of what a Killer Tips book is all about. I can't wait for you to get into it, so I'll step aside and let him take the wheel, because you're about to get faster, more efficient, and have more fun in Maya 6 than you ever thought possible.

Have fun and enjoy the ride!

All my best,

Scott Kelby, Series Editor

INTRODUCTION

Not for the Faint of Heart

3D artists have it tough. They have to wade through seemingly endless amounts of technical minutia from dreary manuals, off-the-shelf books thicker than the yellow pages in a grimy Manhattan phone booth, and well-intentioned but often awkward online tutorials. Then they navigate bleary-eyed through the endless layers of cryptic commands in their applications, wrestling with such terms as "Directed Acyclic Graph," "Non-Rational Uniform B-Spline," and "Non-Manifold Topology." If you can recite the meaning of these terms without forethought, you have already been there! We endure this toil just to satisfy our implacable creative urges to muster up fascinating imagery out of the deep well of technology. 3D animation and rendering is certainly the high ground of computer graphics, pushing one's capacity for technical concepts and jargon to the limit. And, like your grandfather in his youth, mythically trudging through miles of snow making his way to school, we actually LIKE it that way! So, what better reason than to create a book that assembles concise technical tips to speed understanding of the terms, accelerate your workflow to superhuman speeds, and peer into techniques professionals use daily in the visual effects field? When I learned of Scott Kelby's *Killer Tips* series, I recognized that it would be an instant fit in the 3D CGI* world, like beer and pretzels, or in our case, hot pockets and programmers.

Why Maya?

Maya has had an interesting ride into the annals of CGI history in the last few years. It has pounded its way like Mike Tyson into the forefront of professional 3D, and is now considered the standard for 3D work at most of the major visual effects facilities, such as Acme Animagraphics and Industrial FX R Us. Seriously though, it has swept the field, and if there is anything good about that, it is that artists can now carry their expertise and well-earned training with them as they drift from project to project, like the best migrant beanfield workers.

Maya began life as three competing products (Alias, Wavefront, and TDI) that Silicon Graphics had the good sense to purchase and then fuse, Frankenstein-like, into the ultimate über-3D software. Think of it as Einstein's Grand Unification Theory applied to 3D. Or dogs and cats happily romping together. Or Steve Jobs and Bill Gates taking a buddy road trip through the southwestern desert together. In any case, it consolidated many of the separately evolved features that 3D artists had grown envious of. It reduced the prevalent 3D application "camp" mentality somewhat and joined the tribes.

But what secured the success of Maya in the high-end world was that it was the first 3D package to "open the hood" for standard users, allowing amateur

---

*First "TLA," or three-letter acronym, that 3D artists seem to prefer for basic conversation to each other; in this case, "computer graphics imagery."

weekend mechanics (non-programmers) to rummage around in the engine and transmission. So rather than offering an ultimately dead-end tunnel of predetermined GUI* commands, Maya reveals all command structure in text format, allowing clever custom tools to be created (or bumbling stupid ones). Some hardcore Maya users balk at using a GUI at all and type everything. The same crowd would probably prefer punch cards if they were still around, but the option does exist.

Maya also delivers cutting-edge performance in most of the areas it is known for, such as extensive modeling, rich character animation, highly developed dynamic simulation, and a multitude of deformations, as well as offering unique technology like fluid effects, cloth simulation, 3D paint effects, and non-linear animation. Ultimately, Maya has become the "Swiss army knife" of visual effects. Of course, Swiss army knives are not exactly sleek and are fairly cumbersome, and Maya can be seen similarly. Thus, a good understanding is needed to "tame the beast" and coax it into doing your bidding. Alias's early advertising campaign involving a circus lion tamer is not too far off in that regard.

Is This Book for Me?

Absolutely. This book is designed for the advancing intermediate Maya artist, but it will offer gems to all levels. Beginners will find it valuable to clear up some of the arcane mystery of the program, intermediates will use it to add to their growing bevy of techniques, and old dogs will learn a few new tricks to polish off their expertise. The book contains coverage on Maya 6 for users on Windows, Mac, and Linux platforms; however, the screenshots and hot buttons are shown only in Windows. All the tips are applicable for any platform.

Can I Get a Job Working with Steven Spielberg or Jim Cameron After I Read It?

Sure, why not? Stranger things have happened in Hollywood. Steven Spielberg started as a squatter in a studio lot, and Jim Cameron was a truck driver. I would say with that in mind, you could certainly make your mark in Hollywood, armed with the aid of *Maya Killer Tips*. One of the truly great aspects of the visual effects field is that ultimately it is only about your talent. Well, sure, there are SOME power lunches involved, but mastering a difficult package like Maya is a surefire and road-tested route to contribute to the history of the silver screen, and not a bad 8–5 gig if you ask me. Or there's always the beanfield....

---

* Another TLA; in this case, "graphic user interface," affectionately known as "gooey."

Deciphering the Hieroglyphics

SECRETS OF THE MAYA

One's first reaction to opening a session of Maya might be similar to that of an archeologist unearthing an ancient Mayan stone calendar in a remote

Deciphering the Hieroglyphics

unearthing the secrets of the maya

Yucatan jungle. Carefully wiping the dust and pulling the vines away, one knows that the codified icons and glyphs mean something of importance, but what? Similarly, Maya's workflow is not easily deduced from its outward appearance, as it contains many secrets waiting to be discovered by the intrepid and dedicated explorer. In spite of its arcane appearance, however, it is ultimately designed for a fast and efficient workflow. This chapter will introduce you to some of the little-known ways around the program that should speed your productivity and add to your magical aura as a 3D guru. When mastered with version 6.0, you too can feel like a high priest of some secret fraternal order, but luckily without requiring the silly fez hats and robes. You might feel an urge to parade around in miniature cars, though....

HEY, SPLIT IT

One downfall of having everything expressed as nodes in Maya is that the process of selecting them can get quite tedious. The outliner is the preferred method for speed of selection, but what if you are trying to parent a node at the top of the list to one buried thousands of nodes below? Dragging a node to enable scrolling down could take you longer than your lunch break. One often-overlooked enhancement made to the Outliner window is the capability to pull up the bottom edge to split it into two portions, for drag-and-drop speed nirvana….

    USE THE FIELDS, LUKE

Selecting is one of the key Maya skills in life, like learning not to spill on yourself during meals. For those unruly cases where you have 5,000 elements called fooThing0001 through fooThing5000, you could lasso all successive nodes in the Outliner, but it is much more expedient to type this bit of MEL scripting in the Script window: `select "fooThing*"`. Quicker still is to type the same phrase sans the " " into the selection entry field in the main menu strip for ultra-deluxe picking speed!

STRAWBERRY OUTLINER FIELDS FOREVER

Another great place to practice your fields is the unnamed entry bar at the top of the Outliner. Rather than tediously hunting for a particular name nested in an extensive list of nodes, type in wildcards of your choice to limit what the Outliner will now return back to you. Hit the button to the left of the field to return back to the full listing.

TRASH THAT PREF

Even though we want to believe that Maya can do no wrong as a pinnacle of software perfection, every now and then its behavior will get unruly and corrupted, not unlike teenagers. You can perform your own style of troubled teen inter-vention by deleting the userPrefs.mel file that resides in your maya/6.0/prefs folder in the Documents and Settings folder on your drive. You will lose your marking menus and hotkeys by doing so, but it is a small price to pay to help steer Maya down a productive, non-self-destructive path in life.

FIELD OPERATORS ARE STANDING BY

Here is a hot tip for those who have had trouble with basic arithmetic past grade school. Let's say that random transform values are set in the attribute fields of an object, but you are asked to alter it by 147% (150% would be too easy in this case). Rather than take time to break out what my very "old school" engineering professor used to call those new "electronic handheld calculators," you can highlight the field(s) in question and use *=147 to magically multiply all the values by that amount. Other arithmetic operators such as +=, −=, and /= can all be used to avoid that handheld marvel of technology!

NUDGE 'EM

Moving objects around in 3D space quickly is usually not too tough, but carefully adjusting small values to hone them in can be. Rather than fumble with grossly sensitive transform handles, press Alt and then your Up/Down/Left/Right arrow keys to perform surgically precise 1-pixel nudges on your elements— the closest we come to performing delicate brain surgery in Maya. Bear in mind, this will affect all three axes in the Perspective view, while the Up/Down and Left/Right are axially bound in the Orthographic views.

ANNOTATE AWAY

One useful feature you may not have explored is the capability to append text strings to objects in your scene, which serve as virtual post-it notes for your working views. Pick an object, and then choose Create, Annotation to automatically group a target locator and text field node to it, with text editable in the attributeShape node in the Attribute Editor. The text will orient to proper screen space in each view, giving you the ability to clutter up your scene with random daily motivational affirmations or perhaps even useful technical information.

OUTLINER REVEALED AT LAST

Upon selecting an object, one speedy way to locate it in the Outliner under an impossibly deep hierarchy is to choose Outliner, Display, Reveal Selected, whereupon the node is uncovered from the murky depths and revealed in all its blazing glory for all to see.

GET IN LINE, LOWLY VERTICES

Here is a little gem for those cases when a succession of CVs or vertices must align in an axis without losing other alignments. Pick the multiple points, choose Transform with the "w" key, and then click on the shaft of the axis to align to. Make sure that Retain Component Spacing is unchecked in the Move Transform options, and then use a snap hotkey such as grid snap (x) to click somewhere, pulling all renegade points to line up like the Music City Rockettes. If they start a chorus line serenade at that point, consider shutting down and taking the rest of the day off.

SCRUB IT

No, I am not talking about scrubbing your workspace clean, although I have seen enough CG artists' and programmers' environments to know that is not a bad idea. I am referring to the handy but unseen way to scrub values interactively in either the Attribute Editor or Channel Box. In the AE, click in an attribute field and use the Ctrl key and left mouse button to push values up or down on the fly. Try the middle mouse button for a faster response time. Even handier is clicking on the attribute name to highlight it in the Channel Box and then scrubbing your middle mouse button anywhere in a panel view for a true interactive experience. Very handy when the transform handle is hard to distinguish from a dense wireframe behind it.

  ## TUMBLE CAMP

Tumbling through life with default settings is fine for most people, but you know you are not one of them. You enjoy being out on the edge. For you, pushing the envelope of tumbling is where you want to be. Rather than use the default Alt key and left mouse button, invoke the Tumble Tool options under View Panel Menu, View, Camera Tools,

Tumble Tool <options>. First, turn the Tumble Scale from 1 to, dare I say it, one more than 10, 11! Unbridled speed is now yours, and you will dazzle anyone who watches the spectacle. Another nugget is to enable stepped orthographic panel tumbling, normally reserved only for Olympian athletes, but available for the fearless Maya artist who dares tread there.

GOT SPREADSHEETS?

If you were ever envious of financial wizards manipulating great sums of wealth on spreadsheets all day long, look no further. You, the Maya *artiste*, have had your own little spreadsheet in Maya the whole time. It may not make you financially independent, but it will certainly prevent gray hair formation. You can use it to alter a collection of entities from geometry to lights to shaders, preventing the dreaded tedium of manual node-to-node updating. For example, pick a large array of point lights and go to Main Menu, Window, Attribute Spread Sheet to witness all the attributes made available to you in cell format. Now alter a column by clicking in a column header in the top row, punch in a value, and adjust all intensities simultaneously. Not seeing ALL the attributes, such as those in the shape nodes? Simply pickwalk down using the down arrow key once to view all shape nodes' attributes.

Attribute Spread Sheet   _ □ X

Names   Layouts   Key   Help

| Keyable | Shape Keyable | Transform | Translate | Rotate | Scale | Render | Tessellation | Geometry | All |

	Color R	Color G	Color B	Intensity	Use Ray Trace Shadows	Shad Color R	Shad Color G	Shad Color B	Use Depth Map Shadows
spotLightShape3	1.60225	1.12781	0.75477	1.35	off	0	0	0	on
spotLightShape4	1.60225	1.12781	0.75477	1.35	off	0	0	0	on
Key	1	1	1	0	off	0	0	0	off
Fill	1	1	1	0.3	off	0	0	0	off
Fill	1	1	1	0.4	off	0	0	0	off
Fill_Back02	1	1	1	0.4	off	0	0	0	off
Fill_Back03	1	1	1	0.2	off	0	0	0	off

PANEL HOPPING

You may have noticed that when you select a new panel by clicking in it while having an element selected, the panel becomes active, but you lose the selection in the process, not unlike dropping your groceries while leaving the store. An easier alternative than clicking the panel menu bar is to click in the panel using the middle mouse button, which keeps hold of your selected goods, changes the panel, and saves face in public.

IT'S THE RIGHT THING TO DO

Many beginning Maya users will fail to notice things not immediately obvious to them, such as their noses. Beyond that, they may not notice that many of Maya's controls are set up to take advantage of the right mouse button extensively. For example, right-clicking and holding over an object yields a selection mask menu, over the timeline yields all commands relevant to playback and some Graph Editor commands, and over any attribute field yields a full set of keyframe commands. Right-click menus are spread well throughout the package in many more areas, so right-click with abandon!

DRAG-DROP FEVER

Another implementation that may not be obvious in Maya is the drag-drop of node upon node. One classic use of this is to drag one node over another in the Outliner window to parent it below what it is dragged onto. Conversely, you can drag out of a hierarchy into open space in the Outliner to unparent the node. With the Multilister or Hypershade open, drag a Shader Icon directly over some geometry to assign. If you want a new shader created, no need to create it first; drag a shader type from the Create Render Node window on the geometry to assign and create in one step. While working in shader networks, drag various shading nodes onto each other to make connections. Color is the default connection if Ctrl is used, but if you need the Connection Editor, try Shift drag-drop.

LAST ACTION HERO

A very handy key to use when modeling curves or surfaces is the "y" key, which Alias mysteriously calls the "non-sacred tool." Having little to do with anything heretical, it simply completes your tool and resets for another session. For example, drawing a curve is performed by placing many points successively. Rather than use the Return key to complete it and then have to hit the Curve tool icon again, place the last point, hit the "y" key, and you are ready to draw the start point of the next curve. Quite a time-saver for big tracing or curve-generation sessions.

LAST COMMAND HERO

Here is a great little-used key that can really speed up modeling: the "g" or "G" key. If you are creating multiples or doing repetitions of modeling tasks, this is for you. For example, create a primitive cone, move it off of world origin, and then hit "g" to create another. A more interesting variation is "G," where the last action is performed wherever the cursor is located. Hit "G" repeatedly while moving the mouse about and quickly create a forest of cone trees! Create a more complex forest by writing a MEL script that creates a branching tree based on a random seed, and the simple "G" key can quickly rough out a complex environment.

MARQUEE ZOOMING

The dolly command works well for navigating in and out of objects. Alternately, the "f" key fits to a small object, which essentially zooms in. But when you might want to frame a given range or dolly out at a significant speed, try the marquee-zoom trick. Press Ctrl and Alt while dragging a region from upper left to lower right. The framed region is now zoomed into. To reverse out, drag from lower right to upper left.

CHAPTER 1 • Deciphering the Hieroglyphics   **11**

GESTURAL TRANSFORMS

Not a form of pan-tomime, as it might sound, gestural trans-forms are a somewhat forgotten feature developed early on in Maya. Normally, to transform an object, one would use the transform handles or virtual slider described in the earlier "Scrub It" tip in this chapter. A speedier and seem-ingly more magical technique is to select

the object, press the "w" key to enable transforms, and then hold Shift down and use the middle mouse button to gesturally slide the object along an imaginary axis that is roughly aligned to X, Y, or Z. The movement is constrained to the nearest axis, so one can move the object in 3 axes very quickly without selecting any additional commands.

 INCREMENTAL SAVES

Saving is one of the areas that every Maya user has wished he or she had done more often at times. Inevitably, either because of a power outage, BSD*, or file corruption, loud groaning is frequently heard from Maya artists, sounding like something from a

wildlife documentary. One way to prevent this is to use the Incremental Save feature in Maya, found in File, Save Options. Incremental Saves creates an indexed series of backup files during your basic save, enabling you to retrieve an earlier uncorrupted or more suc-cessful version.

The classic Windows system failure, affectionately known as the "Blue Screen of Death."

ROTATION SNAPPING

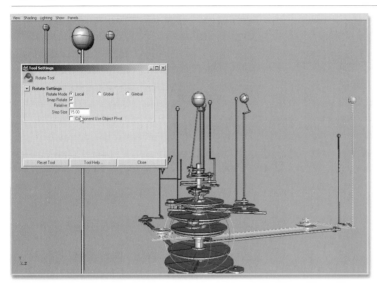

Often when manipulating objects, you need to rotate in fixed increments, especially for architectural situations. In the past you had to tediously input a relative offset rotation in the Field Entry Box. With a recent addition to Maya, you can double-click the Rotate icon on the sidebar, select Snap Rotate and Step Size, and then effectively ball and detent the rotation of your objects. Very helpful when repeating actions for a model.

CLIP IT, CLIP IT GOOD.

Maya's defaults are set up primarily for working with objects larger than a breadbox and smaller than a house, like characters or vehicles. When working with larger items, such as Manhattan Island, the default camera clipping can hide much of your model. Going to each camera's Attribute Editor can be tedious, so use this bit of MEL to expand that default clipping:

```
setAttr "frontShape.farClipPlane" 100000;
setAttr "sideShape.farClipPlane" 100000;
setAttr "topShape.farClipPlane" 100000;
setAttr "perspShape.farClipPlane" 100000;
```

This can be a handy shelf item to have, so look at Chapter 2's "Do-It-Yourself Shelving" tip for shelf-creation advice.

TOOLS VERSUS ACTIONS

Maya was designed with basic precepts in mind, not unlike the U.S. Constitution. One of these basic concepts is that *tools* or *actions* can influence nodes. Many users never learn the difference and thus are surprised by some behavior in the package. The fundamental difference is that a *tool* is active and accepting of input until completed or until the next command is chosen. Examples of tools are the Selection Arrow or any of the Curve tools. Tool options are generally accessed by double-clicking the tool. An *action* is more of a single-shot event made upon a selection, like Lofting or Set Key. Keep in mind that actions often are dictated by the order of the selections, like Edit Curves, Cut Curves. Action options are accessed through the square option box in the menus. These options can be left open to try different settings, unlike tool options. Note that in Window, Settings/Preferences, Preferences under Modeling you can change the behavior of the modeling tools to act as either Tools or Actions, allowing Maya to act like previous software from which you may be transitioning.

RMB SELECTION MENUS

One of the classic "speed traps" in Maya involves having to continually go to the Selection Mask Menus to choose component level entities, such as CVs or vertices. A workhorse of efficient Maya workflow is the selection mask assigned to the right mouse button. As you pass the mouse over an object, right-click for selection menus that give context-sensitive selection depending on geometry type (NURBS or polys). On top of enabling an easy pick of components, you can select the object from there, change display type, assign or inspect materials, and even invoke the 3D paint command for a little touch-up work. Now hold Ctrl and right-click, and selection Grow and Shrink commands are made available for the truly lazy and/or speed-driven.

SLIP-SLIDING AWAY

Sometimes you need more control when moving objects around in your viewport. Oftentimes the manipulator handles are fine, but there are times when you just need better control, whether it's finer or coarser degrees of movement. For example select an object in your scene and bring up the Attribute Editor (Ctrl-A) and navigate to your Transform Attributes. Holding Ctrl down, click inside any one of the Translate fields while pressing your left mouse button (slow), middle mouse button (medium), or right mouse button (fast), and then slide your mouse from side to side to translate your object at varying degrees of speed. Note this does not apply to the Channel Box.

   REVEALING THE INNER OUTLINER

Here's a handy way to get around in Maya's Outliner window, especially when working with a complex character model that has many branching child nodes. In the case of a character scene file, the Outliner window will have many nested objects, which could make it difficult to search through layer after layer to find what you are looking for or just to see how things are laid out organizationally in the hierarchical tree. In the Outliner window, nested objects are displayed with a plus sign centered inside of a square, which you can click to open to the next level. With the addition of the Shift key all the layers of the tree will open, allowing full inspection or organization. Press the plus sign again and the nested objects are neatly tucked away.

SURFING IN A PANEL

In keeping with the modernization effort with Maya, version 6.0 now has a Web browser
function within a working panel. Not really intended to prevent work (though it could excel
at that), the browser can offer some real use for following tutorials or accessing help while
remaining in a work session. Preferences for the browser can be found in Window, Settings/
Preferences, Preferences, Settings, Web Browser, where a home page selection and connec-
tivity options can be set. To initiate the browser in a panel, simply choose Panel, Panels, Web
Browser. Bear in mind that not all the Web functionality you may be used to is supported,
but one new one that has much promise is added: MEL commands can be invoked straight
from a page. This could be a tremendous boon for public sharing of MEL assets or demos,
not to mention the gaming potential.

LAYER THIS, LAYER THAT

The addition of layers to Maya a few versions ago was a welcome feature, but unfortunately it lacked the depth and versatility of what many professional CAD packages offer because their workflow is hinged to layer operations. Now in version 6.0, layers have matured a bit and a few useful new commands have been added. First, create a layer using Layer Editor, Layers, Create Layer, Options. The usual naming field is present, but the addition of an arbitrary number allows reordering from Layer Editor, Layers, Sort Layers Chronologically. Also, note the addition of a new control for adding the selected node or node and children to the layer. Lastly, the addition of Layer Editor, Layers, Delete Unused Layers is handy for automatically getting rid of empty layers.

   ## MAYA ON WHEELS

Some things take a little while in life, like hitting the Lotto or in this case, getting Maya to play well with wheel-based middle mouse buttons, which have been in existence at least since the invention of aerosol cheese. Now unbridled rolling can be had in version 6.0 to expedite zooming in any perspective of orthographic view, Hypershade, Graph Editor, Dope Sheet, Render View, and other windows. But wait, there's more; Wheel-assisted scrolling can now be had in the Script Editor and Console Window. The invention of the wheel is indeed one of man's greatest accomplishments.

BETTER LIVING THROUGH OPTIMIZATION

Optimizing is an essential task and skill in CG, and can often mean the difference between becoming a zero or a hero by the end of a project. Optimization allows large or difficult scenes to be rendered or it can give more room for additional detail or effects for the limited cycles available in a render session. Optimization runs throughout modeling, lighting, and rendering, and can consist of appropriate sizing of maps, for one, or cleanup and deletion of unused elements. Maya consolidates and automates some of the cleanup process by running an optimizing session through File, Optimize Scene Size, Options. Version 6.0 has greatly improved this useful command by adding individual checks, interruptability, faster speed, and better reporting. You might notice a significant increase in parsing time on your renders without the loose flotsam and jetsam of modeling scraps that build up in a project.

REFERENCE AND REFERENCE AGAIN

File referencing has always been a double-edged sword in Maya. It provides a great way to parcel out individual yet consolidated files among a team structure, along with a means to lighten otherwise burdensome amounts of geometry. However, controls for referencing were either limited or clumsy. With version 6.0, file referencing has finally come of age with the ability to load or unload reference files via graphic locators in the construction views, allowing avoidance of the Reference Editor to do so. Start by checking the Group option when using File, Create Reference, Options. This will place the file under a grouped locator along with an editable annotation node. After a few reference files are attached, right-click on the locator, and find the Reload/Unload Related Reference options available for easy turning off and on. The locator will stay visible even when the file is unloaded to allow quick reloads when necessary, all from a modeling window. This will prove to be quite a boon to large and complex scenes.

   SELECTIVE SERVICE FOR FILE REFERENCING

No, not a wartime draft, but rather a very nice feature in version 6.0 that allows the user to choose which reference files are loaded during the opening of a scene file. This speeds read times substantially if certain reference files are not necessary at that point. Start by opening a file containing references with File, Open Scene, Options, and check Selective Preload. After a file is chosen, the Preload Reference Editor window loads. All reference files will be listed with check boxes to prevent loading if desired. Note that loading will be fastest if the file was saved with nothing preloaded, which is accommodated quite easily when saving by checking the Unload References check box in File, Save Scene As, Options. If file referencing has never been part of your workflow, now is a great time to try implementing it.

OVERLAPPING OBJECT WOES

If your model begins to contain a high number of objects that get so tangled up in your model view that selection is next to impossible, this is the tip for you. Go to Window, Settings/Prefs, Preferences, and choose Selection in the Categories column, and then check Popup Menu Selection. Now when you try to select one object out of a jumbled mess of objects, a pop-up menu will appear allowing you to scroll down and make your selection. Improved in version 6.0, the object now highlights upon scrolling to make it even easier to identify.

FCHECK JOINS THE MODERN AGE

Fcheck is a much-beloved remnant of an earlier age when it was macho to not use any GUI assistance at all, but rather to do everything from the command line, which while undeniably efficient lacks some of the common sense of, well, say, the button. Now Fcheck joins the modern age in version 6.0 by incorporating a Control Bar with such advanced controls as Play, Stop, and Frame Per Second (actually difficult to do earlier). Hidden hotkeys such as "z" to show z-depth are now placed front and center as buttons. Fcheck does add a new capability, however, by adding sound support in File, Import Sound, a much-needed addition. For the old-timers who are still afraid to show weakness by using front panel buttons, use View, Control Bar to uncheck and disable its display.

THE DRAG AND THE DROP

There are many times when you'll be asked to build a scene from a library of objects that already exist, and will need to be imported into your scene. Of course you can use the import file command from the file menu and wait for each one to load, or you can try this wonderful trick: Open a file browser and navigate to the location where your models reside to import live. Just select or highlight all the files you want and drag them into a viewport within Maya. That's it—now you should have all your objects in the scene in one fell swoop.

Taming the Beast

CUSTOMIZE IT

3D artists love to gaze at explicit pictures of aircraft interiors, particularly cockpits. Endless banks of needles, gauges, and knobs elicit drool and envy in

Taming the Beast
customizing your interface

most Maya users. Why, you ask? Simply because working in Maya is a lot like flying a 767, albeit a lot lower and slower. We gearheads enjoy rich interfaces with lots of sliders and buttons to push, just to see what happens. I would venture to say that software preference is based primarily on interface preference. So, with that in mind, Maya users enjoy having a lack of boundaries in their software with respect to both function and interface. Alias wisely recognized this fact, and they built what is probably the most customizable interface of any 3D package, carrying this mindset even further with version 6.0. This chapter could easily comprise a book in itself, but I will point out some of the key ways to personalize your interaction with Maya. But be careful, Maya artists can become obsessive in their customization of their GUIs, not unlike some cars with fuzzy dice and curb feelers.

START UP YOUR OWN IMAGE

The first thing we can change is coincidentally the first thing you see in Maya—the startup screen. This is nothing more than free promo for Alias, but you are welcome to replace it with your own little ad campaign, from your kid pictures to your last rendering. Doing so, however, takes a bit of mucking around with some internal files. First, locate the file MayaRes.dll in the bin directory of Maya's install location. Copy this file as a backup, and then use a resource-editing program, such as Restorator, to open it with. Locate MAYASTARTUPIMAGE.XPM.bmp and save this embedded file to disk. Next, edit away in Photoshop, maintaining original pixel dimensions. Now, replace the original with your revised image in the resource-editing program and restart Maya. Now you, too, can have a fully globally illuminated, subsurface scattered, photon mapped, and high-dynamic range lit logo of Maya upon startup, which is sure to be the envy of all your neighbors on the block.

   ### TRUE GESTURAL MARKING MENUS

The Hotbox is a wonderful invention in Maya. Another wonderful invention is Marking Menus. Unfortunately, they don't play too well together, as the true speed attainable in Marking Menus is hampered somewhat by having to call the Hotbox first. If you are not wedded to the use of the Hotbox (some are, some aren't), you can disable it by calling it up with the spacebar, and then selecting Hotbox Controls, Hotbox Styles, Center Zone Only. Now its display is disabled, enabling direct access to gestural behavior from the Marking Menus. To use a Marking Menu gesturally, first hold the spacebar and one of the three buttons on the mouse and make a quick snapping motion in a cardinal direction, which enables the command without ever having to see the label appear from it. After you are used to this way of working, you can never go back, effectively crippling you when you do go back to normal GUI methods, such as helping students or fellow workers at their machines. Lastly, if you do want the Hotbox back, just press Alt-m.

COLOR MY WORLD

Color schemes are another popular way to totally personalize your interface. Color modification in Maya is practically unlimited and can range from a subtle study in tonal design minimalism to an appearance that would make a circus clown happy. Color changes can be made to virtually any entity, from wireframes to background colors. Global color preferences can be modified in Window, Settings/Preferences, Colors, which is separated into General, Active, and Non-active entity categories. The color of individual objects can be set in a multitude of ways. First, select an object, and then go to Display, Wireframe Color for a basic selection from an indexed palette. Next, open the Attribute Editor on the object and locate Object Display, Drawing Overrides. Here, you can change color on a per-object basis. Note that this same override is located on the shape node as well. Lastly, on the MEL side, an object can be selected and changed with this command: `color -ud [color #]`, where color # refers to system IDs of an indexed palette. Finally, to quickly undo any color of an active element, simply type `color`. Doesn't get much easier than that.

DO-IT-YOURSELF SHELVING

Shelves are a truck stop on the road to total customization of Maya— they offer easy setup and access, but they don't quite offer the high performance of a marking menu or hotkey. Maya provides a few shelves that suffice for a starting point, but feel free to delete them and build your own. Use the Shelf Editor to create a new shelf, and then hold Shift-Control-Alt as you invoke a command to add it to the active shelf. You can then MMB-drag them for reordering, inter-shelf mixing, or a one-way trip to the Trash icon at the far right. Remember, shelves are saved in the C:\Documents and Settings*user*\My Documents\maya\6.0\ prefs\shelves directory for easy emailing or transport between job locations. Often, a project-based shelf will be made for a team containing a suite of custom tools for the tasks required. Lastly, the Shelf Tabs consume a small but wasteful strip of screen real estate, so turn them off with the black down arrow pull-down at the far left of the shelf and use the selecting button just above it to alternate between tabs.

   SHELF ICON DECOR

The truly hardcore custom Maya GUI zealots will want to detail their shelf appearances with their own graphic icons and decor. Consider this the interior decoration of Maya. To revise the standard command icon or put fancy renders on MEL script shelf buttons, go to the Shelf Editor, and then choose the Shelf tab to pick the shelf you want to customize. Next, choose the command from Shelf Contents, and then press the Change Image button below. Note the resolution is fixed at 32×32 pixels, and the formats are limited to .xpm, .bmp, and .dib. One possibility is to split a single image into a sequential series of icons that form an image, perhaps of your favorite soap opera star or hair band.

CUSTOM MARKING MENUS—THE BOMB

Perhaps one of the most useful customization modes you can create to speed your work-flow is that of setting up custom Marking Menus. Rooted in MEL scripts, they can be set up for a specific set of tasks for a project or used as the backbone in your workflow. To create one, first create Shelf items of the commands you would like to add. Use "Echo All Commands" in the Script Editor to help display these commands in the Script Editor. When highlighted and MMB-dragged to a shelf, open the Marking Menu Editor in Main Menu, Window, Settings/Preferences, Marking Menus. When there, use Create Marking Menu to MMB-drag your newly created shelf commands to a rosette layout, and then save to the Marking Menu directory in your Maya\6.0\prefs folder in the Documents and Settings folder on your drive. Next, assign each Menu to the Hotbox Center or Hotkey Editor. I prefer dis-abling the Hotbox and setting them in the Center zone, but it is entirely a personal call. For example, highlight a Menu, choose Center Hotbox Region, and put each respective Menu on L, M, or R buttons. Now glory and revel in amazing speed gains, never needing to hunt down your commonly used commands again. Other options for the truly power hungry are to have multiple sets assigned to Hotbox Quadrants or multiple Hotkeys. The danger in all this, of course, is that you will be quite helpless when working on a machine not configured for your soon-to-be neurally embedded configuration.

MY VERY OWN ATTRIBUTES

Maya has so many attributes that you might wonder why anyone would want more. The reason is simply this: One of Maya's most powerful features is the capability to add GUI as needed. You can create custom interfaces to serve very specific tasks that might need isolating into their own menu area for ease of use. You can also extend typical attributes. As a common example, a character rigger might provide the skeleton IK setup and then provide a series of attribute sliders that control a very unique animation that the character might contain. Rather than having to type rotations in XYZ in various default named nodes, the animator might find "ArmSwing" or "ExtendTentacle." If only the 1950's pulp sci-fi's had it this good! To set up a simple example, create a sphere, rename it "Orb" in the Channel Box, and then choose Attribute Editor, Attributes, Add Attributes. Call the Attribute Name "Orb_Spin" and select Add. Now right-click on the Rotate Y field and choose Expressions. In the Expression Editor, type `Orb.rotateY = Orb_Spin;` and complete it. Now look for Orb_Spin in the Extra Attributes of the Attribute Editor and take it for a spin (sorry). Custom attributes are typically rigged with expressions such as this, so brushing up on them won't hurt.

CLICK, DRAG, SELECT!

Sounding a bit like a command barked from a high school gym coach, this is actually a nice way to speed up your workflow if you are moving a lot of elements around. Typically, you first must pick an object and then choose a transform tool on it to move, but this enables a single step for picking many objects in a row without having to reinvoke the tool action. Turn on this little-known feature by checking Window, Settings/Preferences, Preferences, Settings, Selection, Click-Drag-Select.

Now move and arrange, say, a group of bowling pins quickly by clicking and dragging them one by one in succession.

   ## TO GUI OR NOT TO GUI?

For the ultimate GUI (or lack thereof), some Maya enthusiasts turn off all the GUI elements and operate strictly with the panel view and Hotbox. Although this is not a scientifically verified technique for attracting the opposite sex, it can certainly invoke awe in casual bystanders. To turn all GUI elements off, go to Display, UI elements, Hide UI Elements. Note this option is also available by right-clicking in the knurled-looking Stow buttons in each UI component. To restore them, go back to Display, UI elements, Restore UI Elements.

MASSIVE OR TINY MANIPULATION

Transform manipulators come at a default size, but they can be changed on the fly when they become hard to discern by wireframes or various displays. Simply use the + or – keys to scale them up to superhuman scale or down to petite sizes. This can also be handy when a finer degree of manipulation is required temporarily because the larger size can enable finer indexing. To set them at a fixed custom size every session, go to Window, Settings/Preferences, Preferences, Display, Manipulators, and set thicker lines, global sizing, and so on.

   PICK NOTHING, NOTHING AT ALL

Maya is a selection-heavy package—much of its workflow is based on picking this or selecting that. One command that was useful in its predecessor Alias PowerAnimator was Pick Nothing, which deselected whatever was active. Sure, you can click on open space to do that, but often this bit of MEL is useful when used as a hotkey or especially when used for a custom Marking Menu, like in the next Killer Tip. Here is the command: `selectMode -root; select -clear.`

PREFS IN YOUR POCKET

A handy habit of some Maya artists (facilitated by the advent of pocket USB drives) is storing all the customization you have worked long and hard to set up as a series of Maya pref files, found in the Maya\6.0\prefs folder in the Documents and Settings folder of your login directory. These MEL scripts contain all the work you have done with custom colors, Marking Menus, shelves, Hotkeys, and the like. Simply copy these into your new workstation's pref folder, and you are right at home. Also, some artists will carry a resume and current demo reel on the USB drive as well, which is very handy for the "migrant film worker" moving from shop to shop.

   ## WORKING YOUR UNITS

Maya began a previous life as Alias, an industrial design tool. Because Alias was a Canadian company, the metric system was used to describe geometry (a side note, Z is also commonly called "Zed" there, another joint Seussian/Canadian term). Because most industrial design products are smaller than a house and larger than a breadbox, centimeters were chosen as the default grid unit. Larger units can be specified, however, in Preferences, Preferences, Settings, Working Units. Most Maya artists believe it wise not to change these into Imperial units though because basic system calculations such as dynamics, lighting decays, and the like can be altered by doing so. So, if you need to work in feet and inches, consider 1 grid unit to be 1 foot and use decimal conversion of inches for input.

Y-UP VERSUS Z-UP

No, this is not referring to characters from a Dr. Seuss story, but rather the different coordinate systems Maya artists choose to work in. Architects and industrial designers commonly work in Z-up, as CAD systems often default to this system. Film and effects work is almost always done in Y-up, to complicate matters. One simple explanation for the two preferences is that architects and designers tend to work on objects that sit flat on a horizontal plane (thus the notion of depth, or Z, runs up); whereas filmmakers work in a vertical plane (where the notion of depth, or Z, moves away from the camera). Maya can be set to operate natively for either one in Window, Settings/Preferences, Preferences, Settings, World Coordinate System. If you want to convert a model from Z-up to Y-up, simply group the model, rotate –90 in X, and then Edit, Ungroup, with the Preserve Position option checked.

   SMOOTH MOVER

Maya's interactive graphic response is considered one of the fastest of 3D apps, and this is for a few reasons. The Open GL implementation is certainly very robust, but a lot of the speed is attributable to default coarse settings on line curvature and hardware shading samples.

That is generally a good thing, but if you do a lot of precision curve work or find yourself constantly setting NURBS shaded resolution higher than the keyboard stock 3 under Attribute Editor, NURBS Surface Display, Crv Precision Shaded, you can set it globally as a preference, found in Preferences, Preferences, Display, NURBS, NURBS Display. Set Curve Divisions to perhaps 12 and Shaded Divisions to 10. Now Maya will create beautiful-looking objects out of the gate, giving you a luxurious look until you feel a need to place less burden on your graphics card and restore the defaults.

CLICK BOX SIZE FOR HIGH-RES MONITORS

Sometimes selecting objects gets troublesome with curves or thin geometry, especially if you are used to running higher resolutions on your monitor. There is a remedy for this—go to Window, Settings/Preferences, Preferences, Settings, Selection Modifiers and increase Click Box Size from 4 to a higher number of pixels. Set it too large, though, and you will make selections too gingerly, so find the right area for your resolution.

TOP-PRIORITY CLEARANCE

Maya has a dirty secret—it gives preferential treatment to NURBS over polys when selecting overlapping objects. Shocking, I know, but you can actually choose which gets picked first under Window, Settings/Preferences, Preferences, Settings, Selection, Priority. Just pick an entity type, choose Custom Preset, and raise or lower the priority to your liking. Equal rights for Implicit Geometry!

WE DON'T NEED NO STINKIN' DYNAMICS

Another little secret is that two modules in Maya consume an inordinate amount of system resources— Dynamics and Paint Effects.

If Maya starts struggling because of limited RAM, consider turning off these modules, not in the Plug-ins Window as you might expect, but in Window, Settings/Preferences, Preferences, Modules, Load on Startup. If Dynamics or Paint Effects are needed in a scene, or if a command is invoked, they will load, but otherwise Maya will maximize the precious resources you have.

   ## DON'T LOWER YOURSELF TO COMPONENT MODE

Maya is set up to make CV selection in Component mode by default. A crafty bit of MEL can help display these Component level items while in Object mode, thus speeding up your workflow. Type this MEL and make a shelf item, or better yet, a Marking Menu item: `toggle -controlVertex -hull -editpoint;`. You can label it Toggle CV, and you might find it very useful with this Pick CV MEL: `selectMode -component; selectType -allComponents false; selectType -controlVertex true;`. Now all CV manipulation can be done without resorting to the lowly depths of Component mode.

```
// This is the Toggle CV cmd

toggle -controlVertex -hull -editPoint;

//This is the Pick CV cmd

selectMode -component;
selectType -allComponents false; selectType -controlVertex true;
```

MORE AND MORE IMAGE FORMATS

When rendering, Maya provides a basic, if somewhat peculiar, set of presets for resolution and formats in the Render Globals. Sometimes a production team will define a standard for proxy and final renders not found here, so here is little trick to avoid redundant typing when rendering repeatedly. Copy *Maya_Install_Location*\scripts\others\imageFormats.mel into your standard user Maya scripts directory. Then edit this file and add whatever formats you desire. Maya will always read from the users scripts directory first, but just make sure never to overwrite the original install directory scripts, which is generally a BAD thing.

```
//   name                  width height aspect ratio
// --------------------------------------------------
        "320x240            320   240 1.333",
        "640x480            640   480 1.333",
        "1k_Square         1024  1024 1.000",
        "2k_Square         2048  2048 1.000",
        "3k_Square         3072  3072 1.000",
        "4k_Square         4096  4096 1.000",
        "CCIR_PAL/Quantel_PAL 720   576 1.333",
        "CCIR_601/Quantel_NTSC 720   486 1.333",
        "Full_1024         1024   768 1.333",
        "Full_1280/Screen  1280  1024 1.333",
        "HD_720            1280   720 1.777",
        "HD_1080           1920  1080 1.777",
        "NTSC_4d            646   485 1.333",
        "PAL_768            768   576 1.333",
        "PAL_780            780   576 1.333",
        "Targa_486_(tga)    512   486 1.333",
        "Targa_NTSC_(tga)   512   482 1.333",
        "Targa_PAL_(tga)    512   576 1.333",
        "My_Render_Res     2048   898 1.0"
```

PUTTING ON YOUR BEST FACE

When you are working fast the last thing you need to think about is having to slow down to pick a small point on a face, which is Maya's default method for displaying face selections. Sometimes the faces sit so close to one another that they appear to be one, which really makes it tough to select. One thing you can do is change the way your face selection behaves by going into

Window, Settings/Preferences, Preferences, and choosing Selection, Polygon Selection, Whole Faces. This will allow you to click anywhere on the face to select it. If you work with other 3D programs this is a standard method, so it's a good way to keep consistency among your different workflows.

LOADING PROJECT DEFAULT SCENES

Often on very large projects involving a small army of 3D artists, standards are imposed such as render globals, camera film back and gate settings, or common lighting rigs. An artist would frequently have to go locate such a setup file some-

where in order to start a new scene, but new to version 6.0 is the ability to load a project default file as a new scene. Go to File, New Scene, Options, and check Enable Default Scene. You will need to specify the location of said file, but once done, this can be a real timesaver if you are moving through many shot setups with redundant settings. It's the little things in life….

COOL NEW HOTKEYS

Be the first to impress and influence others with your expert knowledge of previously unknown mysterious hidden hotkeys. New to version 6.0 are Ctrl-Space, which toggles the GUI on or off, leaving just the panel to reach its maximum screen real estate. This was previously located in Display, UI Elements, Hide/Show UI Elements, but is now just a flick of the wrist away. Another exotic new hotkey is Alt-B, which quickly changes your modeling view's background color to 3 shades of grey, from the default light, to medium, to dark. This hotkey makes good sense because frequently, different contrast is useful to see and select objects. Now make up a few more hotkeys of your own and bluff coworkers into thinking that they are new additions as well.

A NEW PERSPECTIVE ON TRANSLATING

When using the translate manipulator, a neat trick is to Ctrl-click any of the manipulator axes, which will align the yellow box in the middle to the plane orthogonal to the axis clicked. You can then grab the yellow box and move the object in that plane. The box is set to the plane of the camera by default and can be reset to it by Ctrl-clicking the box itself as opposed to one of the axes. In the example, the default manipulator orientation is being set to the XZ-plane by Ctrl-clicking on the green Y-axis arrow. Note that with scaling, Ctrl-clicking an axis will remove that axis from effect, thus allowing simultaneous scaling in two versus three axes.

COMPARE AND CONTRAST

How many times have you needed to compare values in the Attribute Editor for multiple objects? Too many, right? Well, if you haven't noticed it already, there is a row of buttons at the bottom of the Attribute Editor that can help. In particular, the Copy Tab button comes to the rescue here. Choose the first object whose values you want to compare and click the Copy Tab button, which will create a new copy of the Attribute Editor with this object's values. Then select the other object to load the regular Attribute Editor. Now you can visually compare them.

CONTROL FREAK

Development of proprietary systems in Maya usually involves the creation of nodes dedicated to centralizing control of the system. Some people like to use locators, while others simply create naked transform nodes and then add all the appropriate attributes used to control the system. The point of such nodes is to give the user a one-stop source to manipulate the system (whether at the Channel Box itself or via an interface), so the normal keyable transformation attributes that appear in the Channel Box are generally unnecessary or even downright undesirable. These buggers can be removed by making them non-keyable using the Channel Control window accessible from the Windows menu. Just select the attributes on the left side to make non-keyable and click the Move button. Voila! These attributes no longer show up in the Channel Box. Attributes can also be locked to prevent "user error" by selecting the attributes either in the Channel Box or Attribute Editor, and executing Lock Selected from the right mouse button pop-up menu.

   TOGGLING BETWEEN OBJECT AND COMPONENT MODES

You may often find yourself using the right mouse button context-sensitive menu to switch from object mode to component selection mode to pick individual CVs (control vertices) on a NURBS surface, for instance. But what's an easy way to get back? Using Maya's predefined hotkeys you can quickly toggle modes by hitting the F8 key. Sometimes you'll need to hit it more than once to get to the mode you want, but it's a quick timesaver nonetheless.

USE BOXES TO KEEP THINGS LIGHT

Bounding boxes that is! When you have a heavy scene with lots of objects in the viewing frustum, you can increase refresh times dramatically by setting the display to Bounding Box during camera manipulation. This mode can be toggled on by opening the Shading, Interactive Shading option menu and selecting Bounding Box from the Interactive Shading Mode option menu.

Ah, the glamorous world of modeling. No, not the high-fashion supermodel kind, but rather the more sundry task of efficiently building our base surfaces.

The Glamorous World of Modeling

work smarter, not harder

Luckily for us, Maya is much smarter than your common supermodel. The modeling component in Maya owes its heritage to Alias, which was long considered the industry's preeminent NURBS modeler. Because of this, Maya's initial support was stronger for NURBS and lighter on polygonal modeling, but it is now very robust for both methods, especially in version 6.0. New tools such as Soft Modification and improvements in subdivision smooth Proxy will make even the most jaded NURBS modeler soften up to the world of polys. Thus, here you will find a mixture of useful tips for both sides of the fence. Just remember that modeling is one area of CG production that, if not approached sensibly and lightly, can lead a team into a world of hurt, making the entire project painful and heavy, rather than light and pleasant. So, let's hit the modeling runway—you look FABULOUS!

ALIGNED IMAGE PLANES

Because we frequently use three-view source imagery as a starting point for tracing or guiding our work, a useful technique is to use multiple image planes, each reflecting side, top, or front views, respectively. The trick is to align them properly so that we end up with Michelangelo's *David* instead of your sedentary Uncle Harry. Use View, Image Plane, Image Plane Attributes, Center values to shift the placement of each image plane so that they align with each other. Make sure your original Photoshop images have the same relative scale, or you might end up with your Aunt Edna instead.

ALPHA ONION SKINS

A variation of the last tip is to map a reference image onto a NURB or poly card instead of using image planes. If the reference image is a drawing or is linework-based, copy the Color channel into the alpha in Photoshop, invert it, save it as a TIFF, and then map it with a File Texture to the Color channel in a basic Lambert shader. The alpha will be respected when textured shading is used, turning the card into a transparent onion skin of linework. Next, turn down the Alpha Gain in the File texture node to fade it into the background and align as in the previous tip. Now place them into a layer and use Reference display mode to avoid selecting them during your modeling. They basically become 3D overhead transparencies—a bit more interesting than your garden-variety bar chart, however.

MAYA CARD TRICKS

An excellent strategy for efficient rendering is to augment scenes with scanned images or animated texture maps onto flat surfaces, known commonly as cards or billboards. This is used to optimize an otherwise unmanageable scene or simply to add more detail cheaply. As an electronic version of paper dolls, there are limitations, because the elements must remain roughly perpendicular to the camera and in the background. Cameras cannot roam around them. Good applications, though, would be crowd scenes, trees, cityscapes, or otherwise overly heavy background elements. Note that you must match the lighting in your card image to the scene in which they are being placed, possibly resetting some light direction in Photoshop using the Render Lighting filter. You must also mask out the object, making sure that the area outside the object's alpha is black. Now use this map in an Incandescent channel in a Lambert shader and turn the Color channel down to black. Map a file copy of the Alpha channel to the Transparency channel, which acts as a stencil and creates the look of complex geometry with the expense of a single polygon. Animated maps can be used as well, which are useful for tree leaf rustling or pedestrians walking. This very simple trick is used much more than you might think in many well-known film effects scenes. Just goes to show that the best tricks are often the simplest!

MAPPING VERSUS MODELING

One of the cardinal rules in efficient modeling is never model what you can map. Bump or Displacement mapping can replace surface detail and texture, and Transparency mapping can substitute for excessive repetition of simple elements, such as truss work or piping runs. Distant truss work or piping can be simulated reasonably well using the trick of adding a Bump map of a gradient created by path stroking an airbrush over a truss pattern in Photoshop. This effectively modulates the light normal into a tube-like highlight that otherwise would look flat and mapped.

 INSERT HERE WHILE DRAWING CURVES

Here is a hot tip for modifying NURBS curves as you draw them. As you place CV points, hit Insert before finishing the command, and you will notice it gives you the transform jack to modify the current CV placement. Now press the up or down arrow, and it will move the jack to other points in succession. Hit Insert again and continue, or finish the curve. Pretty tricky, eh?

EXPLICIT, R-RATED NURB TESSELLATION

Sorry, nothing too racy here, just a steamy hot tip that can dramatically speed your renders and reduce your modeling. Maya breaks a beautifully curvaceous NURBS surface into a polygonal mesh during the act of rendering, and it usually does a reasonable job of setting the amount of tessellation required. But as with all automatic things in Maya, it is best for you to decide what is proper. Pick a NURB surface, go to Attribute Editor, Tessellation, Advanced Tessellation, and enable it. If you check Display Render Tessellation in the Tessellation box above, you can compare what Maya is suggesting to a more optimal set-ting that you might make. Use Stick to Mode U, V of Per Span # of Isoparms, and raise and lower the Number setting until that chunky monkey becomes as smooth as a baby's behind. And you thought there was no nudity involved in this tip.

TESSELLATION VERSUS CVS

As we just covered in the previous tip, subdivisions are a necessary parameter to define adequate rounding of NURBS curved surfaces. Many fail to consider, though, that within modeling, the biggest factor affecting render times is subdivisions (tessellation settings) and how they relate to CV count. One can easily magnify the render time by multiple factors if subdivisions are not properly understood.

For instance, many surfaces have a flat component where a subdivision of 1 is all that is necessary. Remember that subdivision settings are relative to the span between isoparms, not the length of the surface. Therefore, if isoparms and the corresponding CV count are high, fewer subdivisions are needed. The inverse is true as well—if you have fewer CVs to describe an object (a good goal), then more subdivisions are required. You can see this is a push-pull relationship, and there are no magic numbers to define just how many CVs are necessary. Typically, it is best to rely on setting finer tessellation instead of adding CVs, which will build up the file size. The main point is to understand what your settings accomplish and optimize just to the point of noticeable faceting, as dictated by the proximity of the object. Setting manual subdivisions is a tedious affair, but if you integrate it into your workflow after each element is built and drink a pot of coffee at each sitting, it goes unnoticed.

LINEAR VERSUS CUBIC HEROICS

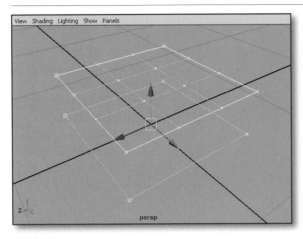

If you envy superhero antics and would like to get similar admiration and respect, try this tip. NURBS models can get notoriously unmanageable in size, often for no good reason at all. In the effort to reduce CV count, a major efficiency step is to use Degree 1 Linear modeling operations over Degree 3 Cubic for flats. The default and often-used setting of Degree 3 creates a minimum of 16 CVs in order to deform a surface freely. Degree 1 restricts the CV count to 4 for a flat planar surface. If the surface never needs deformation and will remain planar (the bulk of architectural scenes or hard models, for example), model with the Degree 1 option. A many-fold savings will result in the weight of your model, creating room for further detail elsewhere. File size will be held down, RAM use will plummet, you will be hoisted up as a true hero, and world peace will ensue (we all hope).

CONSTRAIN THOSE UNRULY CURVES

Here's a handy tip when drawing curves. Maya will constrain the next CV to horizontal or vertical axes with the simple addition of the Shift key. You may have known this since you were in diapers (it's been there since version 1.0), but if not, it's a gem.

THE REVOLUTIONS WILL NOT BE TELEVISED

In our quest to eliminate unnecessary CVs, another very useful technique is reducing the number of sections in a revolve creation. You will notice that as the revolve sections are reduced, the circular profile becomes more oblong and distorted. For entertainment applications, accuracy is not a great factor, so this can be reduced from the default of 8 down to 4, 5, or 6. Also note that the distortion created will only be noticeable at the end profile, so for piping or tubing, it will appear indistinguishable from a higher section element. Again, this will vastly reduce CV count if the model has a fair number of revolves, such as a grimy boiler room containing huge amounts of pipework. Also, it helps to reduce midsection CVs on straight runs by lofting between two circles using the Degree 1 Linear option with 4, 5, or 6 CV circles (not the default 8).

BIRAILING THE MISSING GLASS SLIPPER

If you ever find yourself needing to model a glass slipper for a CG feature animation involving fairy tales (it HAS happened), there is no better way than using the wondrous Birail command. This example is intended to show how Birail can solve some particularly sticky topologies, such as a shoe, by effectively sweeping a changing profile across two guide rails. If you can conceptually break forms down into this scenario, it can work wonders. In this case, draw shoe profiles in the top and side views. Now extrude or loft the side profile curves so that there is a horizontal extrusion that passes over the top profiles. Project a top profile curve onto the extrusion using Edit NURBS, Project Curve on Surface tool. Now pick that Curve on Surface and copy it using Edit Curves, Duplicate Surface Curves. Do the same for the lower profile and attach the side profile curves to the newly created rails. Use Surfaces, Birail, Birail2 Tool to create one half of the shoe. Now use Edit, Duplicate with a negative 1 in the X Scale filed to mirror the other side, giving you a shoe fit for a princess.

SLIPPER REBUILDING

One of the true great Swiss Army Knife commands in your modeling toolbox is Edit NURBS, Rebuild Surfaces. You can change U and V Degree, direction, and number of parameterization spans while retaining the boundary and shape of the surface. This comes in handy when optimizing surfaces or creating the right spans for animation behavior. Let's look at the shoe modeled in the previous tip. Let's say it is too heavy for a real-time game. Turn Spans to 1 and 1 and output to Polygon Quads. This is a NURBS command that often is more flexible to use than the NURBS To Polygons tool. Now let's say that we need to up-res the shoe for a close-up in an ad campaign. Turn Spans up to 20 and 20, output back to NURBS, and we have a gleaming glass slipper worthy of close inspection.

SHADY, UNDESIRABLE ELEMENTS IN MAYA

Maya sometimes provides tools that are initially attractive but end up creating problems in the production pipeline. An example is Trimmed Surfaces, an unavoidable and useful tool for creating odd shapes or holes in NURBS. Trims actually do not reduce ultimate geometry, though. Instead they offer what is in effect a masking of what is underneath. Alternatively, it is useful to create the trimmed surface, use Edit Curves, Duplicate Surface Curves to pull the profile curves, and then Loft or Birail derivative surfaces if possible. Another option is to use the Trim Tool option of Shrink surface. This will reduce the Trim to actual geometry instead of "hiding" it. Holes are a bit more of a problem, but they can be re-created by breaking the surface into discrete patches, or even by trying a transparency map instead. Another problematic command is Surfaces, Planar. A Planar face is a convenient way to create odd perimeters, but it suffers from the same Trim problems. Again, try a collection of patches with a projection map to make up for it, or better yet, use a polygonal surface for such shapes. Lastly, avoid using Edit, Duplicate with the Instance option on. Instances only reduce the working file size of the model, but when going out to render, they don't offer any savings. Therefore, a false sense of security can result as your file grows to unrenderable sizes, even though the file size might be tiny. Worse, Instance copies can create problems when grouping or ungrouping.

RANDOMIZE THOSE CVS

Here is a great trick for deforming objects without deformers. Say what? Actually, this is a very easy way to slightly perturb surfaces without taking the time to tweak a deforming operation. Simply take a NURBS or poly surface that you want to randomize, select all CVs or vertices, and set a keyframe on them. Now open the Graph Editor and use a MEL randomizing script, such as RandKey.mel, found online at a site such as Highend3d.com. With the script, randomize the value, not time, and update on the Time Slider. The surface will be either too subtle or totally wrecked, so adjust accordingly. After adjusting it to your liking, delete the animation on the surface because you will be carrying a lot of animation baggage you don't need.

JUNKYARD DUMPING SIMULATION

Need to model a junkyard with piles upon piles of random objects, all resting on top of each other? You could painstakingly orient each one manually, or you could try this Killer Tip. Take the objects to be piled, raise them up in the air above a plane set at ground level, and with them all selected, choose Soft/Rigid Bodies, Create Active Rigid Body in the Dynamics menu set. With all of them still selected, select Choose Fields, Gravity. Now pick the ground plane and choose Soft/Rigid Bodies, Create Passive Rigid Body. Then play back until the pieces fall onto each other in a jumbled heap, saving you hours of monotony. Aren't 3D apps great? Don't forget to lock down the objects and delete the extra dynamics baggage on the objects by choosing Edit, Delete by Type, Rigid Bodies.

USE OF PHOTOSHOP AS A MODELING TOOL

Photoshop a 3D tool, you say? No, this is not a sneak preview of version 10.0. Instead it's an often-overlooked filter that's been available in Photoshop since version 1.0, found under Filters, Distort, Wave. Sometimes intricate design work needs to be generated for 3D modeling details, and this trick can speed up that process. First, start by drawing basic linework in Photoshop using marquees or lines. Then use the Wave filter with a very small number of Generators, perhaps one to two. Choose Square as the Wave shape, and select Repeat Edge Pixels. You should have a nice garbled and unusable image at this point. To make it shine, turn the Wavelength and Amplitude down very low and tweak as desired. When an aesthetically interesting pattern is formed, this can be autotraced as described in the following Killer Tip and implemented in your model as what the FX industry affectionately calls "Greeblies," or sundry tech details.

AUTOTRACING FOR FUN AND PROFIT

Frequently, we are asked to do things we would rather not do, such as trace the entire shoreline of every continent on Earth. If you are paid by the hour, this might seem like a good deal, but another approach is to automate such menial tasks, which, if I remember correctly, is why computers were invented. Unfortunately, we do have to trace intricate artwork primitively on occasion with NURBS curves, so a rather nice alternative exists using a package designed primarily for graphic artists—Adobe Streamline. After scanned raster artwork is vectorized in this package, most graphics users will fail to see why DXF is provided as an output file type. 3D geeks will certainly see this as a GOOD thing in Martha's words, so at the push of a button, the work of a million monkeys is performed, and all the coastlines are yours in very fine detail (CV count) if desired. Remember that Maya DXF import in version 6.0 requires you to load the Dwg Translator plug-in from Window, Settings/Preferences, Plug-in Manager.

PHOTOSHOP PATHS TO MAYA CURVES

Here's a real magic trick for you Photoshop enthusiasts. Make a path in Photoshop, and then export it in Illustrator format. Now move over to Maya and recall that there was an Illustrator import option. Open the .ai file, and low and behold, it becomes a beautiful NURBS curve, with CVs placed wherever you put a path point in Photoshop. Now here's where it gets really good. Text in Photoshop has a Convert to Work Path command under the Layers menu, so any of the multitudes of fonts you have loaded in Photoshop become yours in Maya. Lastly, the autotracing that the previous Killer Tip pointed out with Adobe Streamline can effectively be done in Photoshop by using the Magic Wand or Color Range tool, converting into a Work Path, and sending the curves over to Maya for more fun and games.

WRESTLING WITH DISPLACEMENT

Displacements are one of the truly great, as well as truly painful, features in 3D. They are a magic bullet for creating detailed modeling that otherwise would be prohibitive or wildly heavy. But there is no free ride in life or CG, and displacements are a good example. Challenges arise when you try to get the exact resolution without artifacts, minimize RAM, and preview to facilitate camera animation. Maya has added Feature Displacement as the default method for tessellating the surface intelligently so that triangles are created only where they need to be. The problem arises from artifacts unique to this method, so you should first adjust Initial Sample Rate to capture the detail required, then start Extra Sample Rate at 0 and inch upward to eliminate noise but retain detail. This differs from the older method of setting explicit NURBS tessellation to achieve detail. Feature Displacement should also help to alleviate the high RAM loads from earlier methods. Finally, to preview results, you need to convert to polygons via Modify, Convert, Displacement to Polygons. The mesh that is created can be only used for previewing, and then it must be discarded or hidden for final renders. If the mesh comes in too large, turn off Feature Displacement in the object's Attribute Editor but check back on render time.

ANIMATE YOUR MODELING

Two animation commands can have great utility when modeling—Animated Snapshot and Animated Sweep. If these are new to you, you are in for a treat. Both are found in Animate in the animation menu set. Animated Snapshot creates a copy of an animated object at selected frames along its performance. This can be used for abstraction or modeling utility if the animation is set up for that purpose. Animation derived from Expressions or IK will not be respected, though, so use Edit, Keys, Bake Simulation first. Animated Sweep differs in that it uses curves only, but its strength is its ability to construct a monolithic surface from the animation. It is conceptually an extrude based on an animated path. Both of these are processing-intensive, but performance can be improved by turning off Construction History.

○ **SET SUBTLETIES**

Grouping elements is typically useful for animation of those elements or for character work. For simple selection and hiding purposes, layers offer a nice GUI. But what if you need to preserve your carefully assembled selection of various objects, lights, and lattices without disturbing their existing grouping? Enter sets, a wonderful way of saving selections without the data overhead of groups or layers. Definition-wise, sets are useful for purposes beyond simple selection, partitions are for exclusive membership, and Quick Select Sets are the preferred type for general selecting. Make your selection and go to Create, Sets, Set/Partition/Quick Select Set. Enter a name, and then deselect the object. Do other work, and then go to Edit, Quick Select Sets, *your set name* to reselect that group without the tedium of carefully selecting a grouping again. Problem is, only you will know how clever you are.

  ○ **TRANSFORM TOOLS SHORTCUT**

Here's a handy little gem when needing to push and pull points or objects around in different orientations. Select an object and hit the usual W, E, or R transform shortcuts, but in this case, keep it pressed, and press the left mouse button anywhere on screen. You are presented with the same options as when you double-click a transform command such as World, Object, or Local Space selection. Quite a timesaver when manipulating points.

INTERROGATING POINTS AS TO WHERE THEY LIVE

Finding the exact location of a pivot point or object center is trivial, but on occasion you might need to find the exact coordinate location of a CV or poly vertex. Make a point selection, open the Script Editor, and type this to call back the X,Y,Z coordinates:

```
xform -q -t -ws;.
```

FACE PROPAGATION VIA SHELL IN POLY SELECTION CONSTRAINTS

I had to use one tip title that sounded pretty technical, so here you are. This is actually a straightforward but powerful trick that can save a lot of hair roots. Pick a poly object, go into Face Component mode, and pick a face. If you now need to pick all connected faces, this can be a chore because of model complexity and/or overlapping UVs. The hot ticket here is to propagate face, vertex, or UV selection using Edit Polygons, Selection, Selection Constraints. When open, choose Shell Propagation and then select Close and Remember. Now pick a face, vertex, or UV, and every one related to that one will be picked automatically. This also comes in handy when trying to separate and manipulate groups of related UVs in the UV Texture Editor.

FAST INTERACTIVE DISPLAY

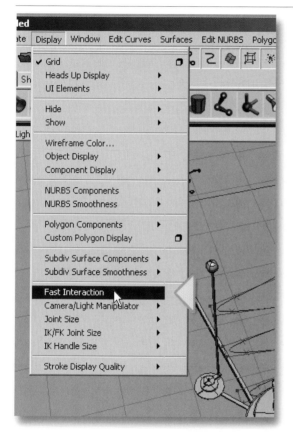

Work faster and more efficiently with large poly models using the Fast Interaction display found under Display, Fast Interaction. Now when you move or tumble around in your scene, things should react faster because Maya will not display every vertex, edge, and face, but a reduced LOD (level of detail) version of your model, and only do so when you are actively moving objects or tumbling your camera around. After you stop, things should display normally again.

FANCY-PANTS DIRECTIONAL SELECTION

If you are paid strictly by the hour, you might want to skip this tip. If you like 100-fold speed increases, read on. Sometimes when dealing with larger scale models like a small city project, you might be asked to delete all the faces from the south side of all the buildings to help lighten the weight of the geometry for better render times. This sounds like good sense, but the effort required will take some time to do. With selection constraints you can do this task in one easy pass, and it will take you no longer than a minute. First select an entire object in object mode, go into face component selection mode, then navigate to Edit Polygons, Selection, Selection Constraints. Under the Constraints section located at the top of the window, choose Current and Next, then check the Activate checkbox in Geometry, Visibility. Now type in 45 degrees for the angle (this is actually 45 degrees from the camera center line, which is the equivalent to 90 degrees). Finally, choose the axis you want to select by placing a positive or negative number in Px, Py, or Pz to choose the direction along the axis you want to select. Now select the restricted faces by marquee-dragging across the entire object and amazing all around you, including yourself.

VERTEX SELECTION FOR ARTISTES

Selecting components of an object such as vertices, faces, and edges can get confusing when you work with objects that carry a large number of faces. Most of the time there's going to be a vertex or a face from the opposite side of the model in that selection that was not meant to be there, and by the time you realize it, you've already made changes to your model that are beyond the point of fixing. Here's one way you can avoid selecting through to the backside of the model and act like a real artiste at the same time. Choose your paint selection tool using Edit, Paint Selection Tool, Options. Notice this is another tricky implementation of the Artisan toolset, so all of the requisite controls are available. If you own a tablet you can even benefit further, and create a masterpiece of painted selection sets.

BETTER MODEL OPTIMIZATION

There are many third-party poly reduction tools available out there, but Maya can hold its own when it comes to poly reduction. The standard method used to reduce the polygon count in Maya is to use the Reduce Tool found under Polygons, Reduce, Options. You can also set the reduction by percentage, but it's not always accurate and things can get undesirable if you go too far. The trick is to use the Reduce Tool in conjunction with the Quadrangulate tool under Polygons, Quadrangulate. For even better results, open up the Quadrangulate Option box and try different settings. This can lead to more successful results, a more organized mesh layout, and the bonus of turning convoluted triangle geometry into nicely organized quads.

TRANSFORM YOUR DUPLICATION

Here is a useful modeling tool, Duplicate with Transform, found under Edit, Duplicate with Transform, or more easily accessed with hotkey Shift-D. Conceptually different from just setting transform values in Edit, Duplicate, Options, this tool allows an incremental amount of transforming to occur as the duplication happens, adding the original transform change onto each subsequent transformed copy. Start by duplicating an object with the standard Edit, Duplicate. Now apply some translation, rotation, and scaling to the copy. Now press Shift-D repeatedly to create interesting derivative forms from the original object.

UNLOCKING VERTEX NORMALS

Here is a hidden gem that is fairly tucked away but has amazing migraine reduction power. In some cases, polygon geometry shows shading problems, exhibiting dark shading partially through a single face, or even inverted face normals within a single object. A situation like this may stem from locked vertices within the object due to an operation like negative scaling or transformations that were not frozen and reset, or perhaps it is just a corrupt model that came from a different 3D package or unknown source. A possible fix to this sticky problem is to unlock the vertex normals with Edit Polygons, Normals, Set Vertex Normal, Options, and then click Unlock Normals.

BEVEL YOUR WAY TO BETTER HIGHLIGHTS

One dead giveaway that something is CG is observing edges that are perfectly razor sharp. In the real world, shy of a razor itself, sharp edges are rarely found. Because every corner has some degree of radius, light catches on these edges and forms small highlights that begin to convince us that an item may be real. These highlights can be done in shaders, or more easily in modeling itself. Generally speaking, unless an object remains at a far distance, you should always have every main profile edge beveled or chamfered. For poly models, this is very easy to do by choosing Edit Polygons, Bevel. If no specific edges are picked, the entire object will be beveled. New to version 6.0 are many enhancements and fixes; most notably, UVs are not decimated as in earlier versions. Now bevels can be added after the modeling phase and used as a way to sweeten and tweak the lighting phase without ramifications. Errors or erroneous results are much more rare in 6.0 as well. A single segment setting of 1 is all that is generally required, as you can dramatically increase your poly count with this tool. For logos and text, NURBS are preferable using the Bevel Plus tool. First create text as curves in Create, Text, Options. Next choose Surfaces, Bevel Plus, Options and explore the extensive range of profile shapes and options. Make sure to use Polygons in Output Options if deformations are planned, as NURBS trims are created, which will tear upon deformation. Lastly, for general beveling in NURBS models, simply build in a small chamfer on your profile curve corners before lofting or extruding.

CUSTOM CURVE MODS

Ok, so you admire custom Honda street mods but only have a Kia? This tip could be useful to at least help you model it. NURBS curves and surfaces have a handy modification tool to allow an alternative to coarsely pushing and pulling CVs. Draw a baseline degree 3 curve and choose Edit Curves, Curve Editing Tool. A gizmo appears with multiple handles to manipulate called Point Position, Parameter Position, Tangent Scale, and Tangent Direction. Move the gizmo at any point along the curve with the yellow square close to the center, and then try some modeling by moving the center square to pull the curve from its original position. Next, move the blue square along the long tangent line to affect weighting Bezier-curve style. Lastly, move the end of the tangent line to reorient the direction of the curve. If you like that, try the same tool on a NURBS surface with Edit NURBS, Surface Editing, Surface Editing Tool. Now you can join the ranks of The Fast and Furious (modelers, that is).

FRESH-BAKED LATTICES

Not an ethnic specialty food, but rather a clever means of modeling, lattices are commonly used for animation but are handy for arriving at complex shapes fairly easily. For example, to model a vase, you could start with a profile curve in order to revolve it, create a default NURBS cylinder, placed lattice around it with F2 (animation menu hotkey), and then use Deform, Create Lattice, Options. Basic divisions of the lattice cage can be entered, but try the default settings. Now, rather than scale the cylinder, pick the lattice, and then select the lattice points under the Component Select Filters (right-click on first Points icon). After the lattice points are active, scale them in Y to create some height. Now select one vertical slice of points, and scale in or out to shape the vase. To see the geometry in decent resolution, you may have to pick the cylinder, and increase the shading precision in its Attribute Editor, NURBS Surface Display, Crv Precision Shaded; try a value of 12–18 or so. When you're satisfied, you can delete the lattice by selecting the cylinder, and then going to Edit, Delete By Type, History.

BRUSHING UP YOUR IMAGE

Here is a pretty slick trick for when you want displacement from an image file but don't want the headaches associated with shader displacement. Create a large NURBS plane with perhaps 100 divisions. Choose Modeling Menu (F3 hotkey), Edit NURBS, Sculpt Surfaces Tool, Options. Known as the Artisan tool, its ability to displace surfaces based on 3D brushes is a very unique and powerful feature on Maya. One method to get more detail on the surface is to use a predefined brush shape under Brush, Profile, Browse. Maya provides a good selection of brush types, but they are nothing more than 256 x 256 pixel 24-bit bitmaps. Browse to an image file of your own, perhaps a DEM surface map. Now you can brush your displacement in a more interactive and modifiable way than using a shader. A given limitation is that the resolution is limited versus a shader solution, but for instances where you need to sculpt the shape without making guesses in Photoshop, it can be very liberating. The final result can also be made into a file for shader displacement by rendering a top view with a z-depth shader or depth map.

INSTANT MUYBRIDGE

Eadweard Muybridge was a pioneer of early freeze-frame photography, using multiple cameras to capture split-second action. This was the seed for what later became a way to freeze time altogether in the *Matrix* franchise. However, you can do a low-budget version of this with the handy Maya tool, Animation Snapshot. Animation Snapshot simply copies the geometry of an animated object at given frame intervals. Start by animating an object, then choose Animate, Create Animation Snapshot, Options. Choose a desired interval and update option, and then press Snapshot. Your model may chug depending on weight, but the result will be a strobed, frozen frame appearance of its performance. Other more practical uses of this tool would be to model repetitive or complex stepping of values in space. Note that dynamics, expressions, and character IK rigging are not supported, so baking of keyframes must be accomplished first.

ALIGNING OBJECTS IN A SNAP

The alignment tool is one of those really useful capabilities in Maya that many artists often overlook. For example, you can align to points on an object, or the midpoint of a face within an object, or even align an object to the center of another object, just to name a few of the options this tool allows. Navigate to the Snap Align tool under Modify, Snap Align Objects, Snap Together Tool, and then select any object from your scene. Now select another object, and there should be a light blue line displaying the trajectory of the first selected object to be aligned and snapped to the second object in your scene. By default when you pick an object, it will snap to points on the object, but by going into the tool's options, you can snap to a poly face instead. Also note that it is worth exploring the various other Snap Align tools in the Modify, Snap Align Objects menu.

NURBS NOW CONVERT TO SINGLE MESH

NURBS patch models are great to work with, except when you have to convert them to polygons. NURBS are usually comprised of many surfaces that form an object, and when converted to polygons, you're left with many objects that will need to be joined together. Thankfully, version 6.0 has added the ability to do all this in one step. Under the Modify, Convert, NURBS to Polygons, Options menu is a new checkbox labeled Attach Multiple Output Meshes. Checking this box converts your NURBS to polygons, and then attaches all the surfaces together to form a single mesh of wondrous 3D goodness.

KEEPING SCALE WHEN WORKING WITH UVS

Scale is very important when laying out UVs, especially for architectural models. One example of this would be a brick building. If various texture UV scales are off even slightly, the bricks will appear offset from one another. A great way to be sure your UVs are in scale to one another is to place a slightly larger cube around your model. When you select faces to UV, be sure to add the face of the cube that's closest to your selection. When you are finished placing UVs on all sides of your model, arrange your UVs accordingly.

AUTO MAPPING MOVE AND SEW

Maya's UV Editor has many powerful features, one of which is the Move and Sew tool. Move and Sew allows one to stitch UV coordinates together to form a single unwrapped UV layout. When dealing with rectilinear geometry, a great way to quickly unwrap the model is to use the Automatic Mapping texture coordinate system in conjunction with the Move and Sew tool. This will create a clean and properly scaled UV layout. It doesn't get much easier than this.

MIRROR CUTTING

When working with architectural models it is very common to model a ledge or cornice that wraps around the façade of a building. It usually has a mitered corner, and unless one knows the trick to scale the cross section 1.414 times and rotate it 45 degrees, it can sometimes be difficult. With the Mirror Cut tool, found under Polygons, Mirror Cut, that all goes away. Just specify what axis to cut on and it will mirror your geometry perpendicular to the cutting plane. The cutting plane can also be rotated at any angle and the geometry will continue to conform to it.

ALIGN TO UV SPACE

Alias has done a wonderful job expanding the toolset found in the UV Editor. There are many new features, one of which is the UV Align tool. Now you can select points in UV space and align them to other points in UV space. No more aligning by eye; this new tool makes aligning points quick, accurate, and a real pleasure to work with.

WHAT'S IN A NAME?

As trivial as this may sound, I can't stress enough the importance of naming objects appropriately as you create them. If you're working on your own, it's up to you as to how you want to organize yourself but if you're working in a production environment, it's of utmost importance to talk with others to decide on naming conventions for the show. Producing scenes full of Maya auto-named objects is a sign of poor style and is unprofessional. You'll get a lot of grief from people down the line trying to write scripts that count on naming conventions to parse the scene file to perform some sort of operation using the geometry you've modeled. There are a few options in Maya to help you organize yourself and your data. One is the use of namespaces. They allow for parallel object constructs so if you have, for instance, a group of fighter jets in formation, each jet can be an exact copy of the original, differentiated by its namespace. Namespaces are identified by a prefix followed by the ":" character. One way to create namespaces is to have the base object saved in one scene file and then import it into a new scene file with the Use Namespace option checked in the File, Import dialog window. Also set the Resolve option to "all nodes" and set the With field to "this string:" and finally enter the name of the namespace in the text field. This can be done as many times as needed, with each import having a different namespace specified. Another tool is the Modify, Prefix Hierarchy Names menu item. You can quickly distinguish collections of objects by renaming them all with the same prefix. This is also a mechanism to move objects into a namespace by using the namespace name plus a ":" character.

SURFACE PARAMETERIZATION FOR REBUILDING

One of the greatest advantages in working with NURBS is the ability to sculpt organic-shaped objects, like asteroids, tree trunks, and terrains, just to name a few. With NURBS, the UVs are established automatically. However, in some cases where the surface gets pushed or pulled to extremes, surface parameterization will suffer and textures will appear stretched. A good tip to help minimize these overly stretched UVs is to build a better-parameterized surface. For example, create a NURBS sphere and with the Sculpt Surfaces/Polygons tool found under Edit NURBS, Sculpt Surfaces Tool, paint a displacement onto the NURBS sphere. Select some control vertices (CVs) and move them around to form some extreme angles. Apply a grid texture onto the object, and notice how the grid texture will warp undesirably to the object, especially around the areas of extreme shape variations. Now duplicate the curves from the NURBS object by selecting the object first, and then navigating to the Edit Curves, Duplicate Surface Curves, Options. Select U or V from the options window; for this example, check the U box. There should be a series of curves placed over the surface; move them beside the original surface for ease of viewing. The next step is to loft across the newly created curves. Select Surfaces, Loft, Options. Be sure to select Chord Length from the options menu. Apply the grid texture to the newly parameterized object, and compare the quality of the texture to the original object. The Grid pattern should appear more regular in scale on the newly created object.

SOFT MODIFICATION TOOL

Whether modeling a character or any other organic object, the trick has always been to move vertices around in such a fashion that faceting is kept to a minimum. A common method is placing a lattice around the region you want to influence; this is fine for larger areas. With the Soft Modification Tool new to version 6.0, you can target specific regions of the object and scale up and down the amount of influence as well as the type of smoothing interpolation to apply (none, linear, smooth, and spline), thus giving much more control. The Soft Modification Tools menu can be found under the Modify, Transformation Tools, Soft Modification Tool. For every control point placed onto the object, a new control node is added to the outliner that represents each point. Feel free to name them, and if double-clicked, a detailed options menu will pop up, giving separate control parameters for each control point.

GET RID OF THOSE STEALTHY, HIDDEN VERTICES

When building a scene from scratch, it's common to import models from a third-party or other outside sources. Due to many different 3D software programs available today, models are usually exported to other 3D packages with a commonly accepted file format. Obj has been a standard format for many years, and is regularly used in the 3D community. Because there are so many 3D packages available, not all deal with data the same way. A good example of this would be to export geometry from Maya to an Obj format, then import it back in. The file should be clean, but if this same geometry were exported from another 3D package, then imported into Maya, it's possible that it may have inherited duplicate vertices. To check this, enable the Heads Up Display (HUD) option found under Display, Heads Up Display, Poly Count. This will now display selected geometry information directly within the viewport. Duplicate vertices are visibly undetectable but are very noticeable when it comes down to performance and file sizes. If you suspect that the vertex count is suspiciously high through the HUD, try selecting all the vertices in that object, then delete them—if there were duplicate vertices, the vertex count should drop. This should not affect the original geometry, just the duplicate vertices.

SMOOTH YOUR PROXY

One of the more commonly used methods for modeling a character is to model either the left or right half of the character, then mirror the geometry to create the opposite side, then finally merge the vertices together. With Smooth Proxy for version 6.0, you can apply a mirror option to create symmetrical geometry that is then mirrored to the other half of the model, making symmetrical modeling much faster and easier (multiple times faster than in version 5.0). For example, create a box, subdivide it a couple of times, and then delete half the box on the X axis. Select Smooth Proxy from Polygons, Smooth Proxy, Options. In the options menu, set the Mirror Direction and click Smooth. Begin modifying one half of the smooth proxy, and the opposite half should automatically update.

SET THOSE FACE NORMALS STRAIGHT

When geometry is imported from another 3D package, it's quite possible that normals will come in flipped or locked for that matter, and trying to reverse them will not always work. For those cases where faces appear to be reversed but don't seem to toggle back when the reverse normal command is applied, try the Set to Face command under Edit Polygons, Set to Face. This will unlock any locked face normal and set the normal direction to match the rest of the geometry normals. Note that if you had any smoothing applied to the geometry, you will have to reapply it because the Set to Face command will remove it.

Embracing the Revolution

Lighting in Maya is, ironically enough, a "dark" art—there just aren't any cookbook recipes to follow. If you gave 100 Maya artists the same task to light a space or character, you would probably end up with 100 different

Embracing the Revolution
lighting your way

results. Of course on a big project this could pose a major problem, so teams spend time creating standard rigs and approaches, but in general lighting is more an intuitive art than a standardized craft. It is responsible for the success of a scene more than any other factor, but above all it is just plain difficult. Adding to that difficulty is the fact that of all CGI technologies, it has been the most difficult to create photorealism with lighting because of the crudeness of the tools available. However, a major revolution is underway—Global Illumination. With version 6.0, Mental Ray now offers the richest opportunity for GI lighting in Maya. GI offers a simulation-based approach to lighting that is light years ahead in terms of accuracy, though it sacrifices a bit of the carefully sculpted lighting of the artist. Whereas most 3D development is evolutionary, GI is revolutionary, and it is rewriting all our long-standing methods. We are currently in the middle of this revolution, so luckily older and well-proven approaches are still valid because the new ones are being put into serious production stresses. Therefore, you will find Killer Tips on both sides of the lighting movement in this chapter. Viva la revolucion!

TWEAKING LOTS O' LIGHTS

Undoubtedly you have created vast multitudes of lights (Maya artists LOVE lights) and had to globally change them for some reason or another. Rather than progressively altering them individually in the Attribute Editor, try the Attribute Spread Sheet. OK, maybe you have tried that, but what if you need to change all the more obscure attributes, such as Shadow Map Resolution? You may have found those attributes are missing. The trick is to use the down arrow key to select the Shape nodes and load all the previously hidden attributes under the All tab of the Attribute Spread Sheet.

REUSE THOSE DEPTH MAPS

Maya has gotten very quick at calculating Shadow Maps, but over the course of thousands of frames, all that calculating can add up. If nothing moves substantially in your scene or background, consider Depth Map Shadow Attributes, Disk Based Dmaps, Reuse Existing Dmap(s) in the Attribute Editor of the light. This will write out the maps into *Your_project*\renderData\depth directory. They will not be deleted, as is the norm, and they will be reused for every frame. This can substantially cut down your renders if the shadow can stay still. For a character that moves, consider a linked light, which calculates on every frame. Lastly, remember that these depth maps can be inspected with Fcheck and the "z" key, which is very handy when trying to debug shadows.

COOKIES AND GOBOS

Sounding like something yummy from your childhood, these are rather old Hollywood terms for ways of manipulating the spread of light. Cookies and Gobos are actually paddles or cards with random holes cut out to deflect key lights into a draping of light and shadow or to soften the spread. Defining the signature look of the Film Noir period, they are useful for dramatic effects or simply for enriching a scene. Cardinal Rule #1 in CGI is that *Imperfection Is Your Goal*, so here is a great way to emulate that technique using a simple CGI Spot light. First, paint a few random black and white organic patterns in Photoshop and save out as a TIFF file. Now create a Spotlight in Maya, and in the Attribute Editor, map a File Texture to the Color channel. Choose a Gobo file of your choice and adjust Filter Offset in the Spotlight Attribute Editor to add blur and softening to the sharp contrast. Adding warm hue into the Texture File Color Gain and cool hue to Color Offset can create further interesting effects.

without gobo

with gobo

LIGHTING WITH PAINT

Allen Daviau is one of Hollywood's top directors of photography. An interesting statement he once made is that he often not only "paints with light" as the saying goes but also "lights with paint," using stage painters to attenuate surfaces into proper exposure. Conceptually, we do the same thing with our shaders. Lighting is inseparably intertwined with our surface properties. One shader attribute that has great usefulness to lighting is Incandescence Mapping. This is a terrific method to add or replace the appearance of lights. It is limited though because it doesn't offer a lighting solution for objects per se but is simply an illusion or painting of light appearing in the scene. The Incandescence attribute channel of a shader simply takes the color map and renders it at full (or at a potentially partial) value. The trick here is to use a painting program such as Photoshop to pre-paint the lighting onto a simple render or screen grab of the surface. In Photoshop, the Render Lighting filter is very useful; just keep the Ambient slider set to zero in that plug-in. For architectural scenes, it is a great way to simulate the appearance of hundreds of lights without even containing a single one, as the almost entirely incandescent mapped example shows.

KILL THAT AMBIENT!

I don't normally condone violence, but there is really no place for ambient lights in good CGI. A better solution is to create a Directional light cluster by copying a handful of six or so Directional lights and placing them into a grouped cluster around a single pivot. Now rotate them counter to your main key and begin to rotate them apart, effectively giving light from multiple directions but enabling the etching of the sculpted form to occur, which a stock Ambient light naturally kills. The trick of course is to keep intensities down enough to not notice their directional sourcing. One option is to turn off the Emit Specular component in the light Attribute Editor.

CUBIC POINT ARRAYS

Another great way to avoid the evils of Ambient lights is to use an array of cubic decay Point lights. In the case of lighting an interior space, Ambient light will unify everything into a monotonous flattening. A collection of Spot lights can accentuate certain forms but doesn't really offer a way to do an overall space. Area lights are best for this task, but they can drastically increase render times. A good compromise that offers more flexibility and a GI look is to fill the space with overlapping spheres of quickly decaying light provided by Point sources. Effectively a manual setup of an Area light that is tailored to the space, this method almost always provides a good solution for roughing out an interior scheme. Begin by placing an array of Point sources vertically midway from the ceiling to floor and spaced at that same distance apart. You may end up with rows of lights to fill the room, perhaps up to 20 or 30 lights. Adjust the intensity to equal a net level of 1.0, that is, 10 lights at intensity 0.1 for each. The key here is to use the highest rate of decay—Cubic. The intensities will run very high (about 2000), but they are abstract. With the fast falloff, pockets of shadow will accumulate in the corners, mimicking a GI render with a fraction of the render time. Additional Spot lights can be added for warm or cool shifts and accents on interior elements. A weak Directional light can be used to pull forward any wall that may need accenting over others. Note we have used no Ambient lights in this strategy. Lastly, don't turn on Shadow Maps on these Point lights, which is explained in the next Killer Tip!

FEAR OF POINT LIGHT SHADOW MAPS

One thing that many artists overlook is that using shadow maps on a Point light does not generate one map, but six! As shadow maps are effectively renderings taken from a point in space to cover a 360-degree area, Maya adds six hidden spot cones, rotated 90 degrees to each other about the Point light center. Each cone angle's coverage is 90 degrees and is square, providing a full surround. Maya is considerate enough, however, to provide a way to turn off these maps under Depth Map Shadow Attributes, with check boxes for Use XYZ+– Dmap. Not that you can't theoretically run 120 shadow maps on 20 lights on a render (though it's probably not a good idea), but now you will know why your box sits there for hours, lost in thought before even rendering a pixel.

LIGHT COLOR MAPPING VERSATILITY

A valuable aspect of Maya lights is the capability to map the Color channel in the Attribute Editor. This simply places an orthographic section cut of your Spot light's color pixels with a rectangular or solid map of your choice, and it offers potential for many varied effects. First, it is useful for custom-designed penumbras. Apply a 2d Ramp Texture node to the Color channel of the light and create a grayscale circular ramp. This acts as a secondary means of controlling the falloff of light within the penumbra already set by changing the effective light color out from the center. Another common use is to assign a 2d Fractal Texture node to the color but adjust for low contrast, so that the even light is randomized to a slight "blotching." If done subtly, this introduces a scale factor and rich irregularity to cast light. The next obvious use of this is to connect a 2d File Texture node, acting as a slide projector of sorts. Lastly, the look of multiple lights can be simulated with one light by mapping a 2d Grid or Bulge Texture or a repeated circular ramp to give the appearance of a light passing through a diffuser. If Shadow Mapping is turned on together with Light Fog, multiple beams will be defined, giving you an instant disco!

POOR MAN'S GLOBAL ILLUMINATION

In the constant quest to achieve the look of Global Illumination without the associated exorbitant render costs, many have adopted the use of hemispherical layouts of traditional Spot or Directional lights. Web sites such as Highend3d.com have some excellent rigs available for download, such as GI Joe. If you feel ambitious enough to make your own, create a poly sphere with a Subdivision Axis of 8 and a Subdivision Height of 6. Delete the lower faces to leave a dome. Create a Spot light, scale to .1, and then snap to one of the vertices. Turn on the Manipulator Tool in the Toolbox and grid snap the focus point to 0,0,0. Copy the light to the next highest vertex and reposition its focus back to 0,0,0. Center each light's pivot back to 0,0,0 and use Edit, Duplicate to copy the two Spot lights 7 times with a 45-degree Y rotation. Group the Spot lights, delete the sphere, and turn on Shadow Mapping with 1024 Map Resolution. Now export the dome as active and import into a scene. Scale up the top node of the lights while choosing Panels, Looking Through Selected on a single Spot light to maximize the area covered by the Shadow Map. Render away, and you get a poor man's version of GI shading. For a middle-income version, try GI Joe, where an environment map can inform each light's color for a High Dynamic Range (HDR) fake, and the number of lights used is far higher for smoother shadowing. For an upper-crust earner, try true GI and HDR rendering in Mental Ray. Expect to pay for the privilege, though.

HDR GI CGI TLA

High Dynamic Range is more than another of those geeky three-letter acronyms (TLAs); it is a fantastic way to match CGI into photographic backgrounds using photography itself to act as the only lighting source. At its highest implementation, it relies on Global Illumination raytracing to provide all lighting and shadow into the scene, albeit at a costly rendering expense. HDR can be faked somewhat using GI Joe, mentioned in the previous Killer Tip, but now that Mental Ray is native in Maya, the doors are wide open. To start, acquire an HDR file online, such as those found at Debevec.org. Open Window, Settings/Preferences, Plug-in Manager to check to see if Mayatomr.mll is loaded. Create a sphere and scale it up well past the scene you have created. Now create a Lambert shader, and assign the HDR image to a File Texture mapped to both the Color and Ambient color channels. Make sure your scene objects have Blinn or Phong shading models, as you need reflectivity attributes. Render using Mental Ray, and turn on Final Gathering. Use Draft quality to check results, then try Production quality around the time to take a dinner break. New in version 6.0 is a shortcut for this process. In Render Globals, locate Image Based Lighting under the Mental Ray tab, then press Create to set the entire process up automatically.

PAINT THOSE SHADOWS

After all that previous discussion on snooty high-brow rendering technique, let's dumb it down (in a good way). Shadows can actually be cheated in a very easy and successful way by painting them in. There are various ways to accomplish this, from painting them into textures to creating shadow planes under objects. Let's look at a great way to add them where you need them using Layered Shaders. In this illustration, soft shadows were required for the beams overhead in this Native American kiva. Rather than use expensive GI, a Layered Shader was constructed with layers of soft shadow images created in Photoshop. Started by screen capturing the top view of the elements, it was pen-path-stroked by an airbrush in Photoshop into a clean layer and saved out as a TIFF file. The Layered Shader in Maya effectively composites the multiple layers, and it can mix shading modes like Lambert and Blinn onto the same surface. Use of Lambert for the shadow layers prevents unrealistic specular washes in the shadowed areas. Shadows on the walls are added by applying a 2d Ramp Texture to the Color Gain of the 2d Texture File, multiplying it down toward the ceiling. Lastly, the woven bowl and structures on the floor have shadow plates below them, to be discussed in the next tip.

SHADOW PLATTERS

Pronounced Shadow "Plaa-tairs" in French, this highly advanced tip will challenge even the most astute Ph.D. (another TLA). Okay, here we go, try to follow: Create a NURBS or poly plane, position it just above the floor surface and below your shadowing object, and attach a Lambert shader. Make the color black and map a 2d Ramp texture to the Transparency channel. Make the ramp circular or boxed, add a bit of Noise in Ramp Attributes, and render away. You are left with a beautiful soft shadow with virtually no render overhead. If your geometry is complex like this pile of boulders, render it from top view and use a blurred alpha channel instead of the 2d Ramp Texture. Remember to turn off Casts Shadows in the shadow plate's Render Stats in the Attribute Editor. Tough, huh?

GLOWS, FOGS, AND FLARES, OH MY!

Maya lighting has the unique capability to simulate optical properties such as Glows, Fog, and Flares. These are quite useful in digital sets for their capability to simulate atmosphere and add presence to a scene. The use of fog to cast a visible spread of a spot, coupled with radial Flares or Glows onto the light, adds a great subtlety that contributes to the realism of the scene. Careful use of these effects is necessary, as they do have some pitfalls. First off, Fog effects are always preferable to Glows for a few reasons. Glows and Flares are a post-process render step, which can require large amounts of RAM and additional render times. If Fog effects are set up correctly, they can often match the look of more expensive Glow effects but result in fewer problems due to their true 3D world space description. Also, Glows can flicker on small objects annoyingly due to eye space auto-exposure calculation errors. A setup combination of dummy lights not casting light but contributing Flare, Fog, or Glow components can add greatly to the scene. Often these can be pre-rendered and mapped onto a card using Incandescence Mapping. Or keyframe some animated 2d Fractal Noise into the Color attribute of the Fog, and a convincing atmosphere is guaranteed.

SHADOW MAP WOES

Shadow Maps (Dmaps) are a necessary evil in 3D. They are often fraught with instability and artifact issues, but their low impact on render times makes them necessary bedfellows. The default settings of a Spot light Dmap in Maya produce fast, soft, but not very accurate shadowing. To establish harder or more accurate shadow edges, it is necessary to adjust the parameters of Cone Angle, Dmap Resolution, and Dmap Filter Size. Typically start by narrowing the Cone Angle as small as possible, and then increase Dmap Resolution. If a softer look is required, try to increase the Dmap Filter Size, but beware of long render increases. Realize also that RAM use will rise dramatically with higher resolutions. For more accurate start points of the beginning of the shadow, or to reduce shadow artifacts, try a larger or smaller value of Dmap Bias. For greater stability in animations, always turn off Use Dmap Auto Focus and enter the cone angle value here. Often a certain combination is required with these settings, so render only on a selected few objects to test on and arrive at these settings quickly.

USE OF THRESHOLDED SHADER GLOWS

Shader Glow is a common effect added to a surface that aids the appearance of self-illumination, such as a glowing television screen or car headlight. It adds the appearance of the "blooming" of light due to high contrast or strong intensity. The problem arises as the entire surface equally glows by default, creating the look of an unfortunate nuclear accident on that to which you apply it. A little-known control exists in the Shader Glow global attributes, found as an extra shader ball in the Multilister or Hypershade. Locate Threshold in the Common Shader Glow Attributes, and you will find that as it is raised, only the specular highlights will then bound the apparent glow effect. The end benefits of this technique are to show a light blooming effect in your renders and impress others at cocktail parties.

DANCING FIRELIGHT

Here is a great, simple trick for animated light from a campfire or candlelight. Place a Point light in the center of your flame and keyframe a rich, saturated color for the starting frame. Advance to the end frame and set a key. Now open the Graph Editor and add multiple keys across time in all the RGB curves present. Locate a randomizer MEL script, such as RandKey.mel found at Highend3d.com, and use it to randomize all the intermediate keys you just created. Now, because the keys on each of the curves are diverging from each other on the R, G, and B channels, the lighting will change color temperature and intensity during playback, giving an eerie life to the fire that you have rendered.

   LINK THOSE LIGHTS

A useful technique to use for greater efficiency or just to get you out of tight places is light linking. Light linking enables a surface to be solely lit by a particular light, effectively pulling it out of the scene. This should be used judiciously, as the scene can quickly look unnatural. At times, though, it is useful for setting up a lighting effect that cannot occur with standard CG direct illumination lighting, such as light transport phenomena of bouncing or washing around objects. To use light linking, select the surfaces and lights desired and choose Lighting/Shading, Make Light Links from the Rendering menu set. Selecting Window, Relationship Editor, Light Linking gives you the ability to inspect connections and choose Light Centric or Object Centric, enabling flexibility in which is attached to which.

SHADOW LIGHTS

Possibly one of the most useful lighting techniques I use, Shadow lights are indispensable once you get used to them. They effectively enable you to place shadows independently of your lighting, something that a more flexible renderer such as RenderMan excels at. They also are very easy to set up and use. Start by creating a Directional light to provide the general key lighting. Next, create a Spot light of Intensity 1 and turn on Shadow Mapping. Adjust the Cone Angle and Penumbra Angle as you might want it for shadow purposes. Duplicate this light in the same position, but turn off Shadow Mapping and put –1 for intensity. The light components cancel each other out, leaving only the shadow. Group the two together and throw shadows exactly where you want them at any resolution. This is an excellent tip for large scenes where the Shadow Map gets too diffuse for the scale involved. Lastly, try Matt Wood's MWShadowLight.mel from Highend3d.com; he has made it plug and play by writing expressions between the key Attributes of the two lights. Shadow on!

LIGHT CYCLES

No, this is not a reference to *Tron* (that is if you are one of the three people who saw it) but rather a cool feature of Spot lights that may have slipped past you. Select a Spot light and hit the Show Manipulator Tool below the Scale button on the Toolbar, or better yet just hit "T." You are presented with the focus and pivot locators for the light, which is handy in itself, but you may not have noticed the tiny clock icon to the side. It is the Light Cycling Index, a fancy name for a button that cycles through different interactive adjustments for the light, from cone and penumbra width to decay regions. Now use Look Through Selected on the light and notice that it has added interactive barn door edges, making that task very speedy when lighting your homage to *Tron*.

SPOTLIGHT DECAY REGIONS

Spotlight Decay Regions are handy when you need well-defined foggy searchlights to light from lampshades. Use the Light Cycling Index mentioned in the previous Killer Tip to display an interactive series of rings that define the borders of where light will occur. Adjust them so that the light begins outward of the origin of the cone so that light and fog are not revealed until appropriate.

CONSULTING SUN CHARTS

In film work, we are constantly combining CGI with photographic backgrounds, or "plates." Matching up the lighting so that it is seamless is the real work. It all starts by determining where the sources were during the shoot. On a stage, this can be found by analyzing all of the measurements and survey data usually recorded. But what if the shoot took place outdoors, with the sun as the primary available light source? Some packages have coded in the ability to enter time of day, year, and location to re-create the sun vector direction, but Maya has not added that feature yet. In the meantime, use what architects use to determine solar angles—a sun chart. These can be found online or in solar energy guidebooks. Follow the time of day and year to locate the associated bearing and azimuth angles, and then use those to set the rotation of your key light. Shadows and highlights should now play well with each other. This is an inevitable MEL script to be written—any takers?

DIRECTIONAL SHADOW MAPS

The use of Shadow Maps with Directional lights poses a problem. They look good, as the shadows look more uniform and parallel, but it is often very hard to get decent resolution. It is not hard to see why if you realize that the spread of the map is applied based on the largest object in your scene. It you are rendering a still life of a bowl of fruit, that is fine, but if you are rendering the island of Manhattan, one shadow pixel may spread across a street. Luckily, Maya gives us an option to apply a reduced cone angle to the spread, Use Dmap Auto Focus. Uncheck it and key in a smaller number, based in degrees from the centerline of the directional. The Directional light now begins to act like a Spot light, so position matters for proper application of shadows. The Use Light Position switch uses the location of the light to determine if objects behind or in front are considered in the shadow map. If lack of resolution still poses a problem, consider using the Shadow light technique described in a previous Killer Tip in this chapter instead.

SEE YOUR SHADOWS

When lighting a scene, it's often difficult to see how your lights are behaving in your actual scene until you go to render it. More often than not you will have to readjust your lights because the shadows being cast are working against your well-earned composition. How great would it be if you could see your shadow in real time in your viewport so you could make all those crucial adjustments beforehand? Look no further, hit 7 (use hardware lighting), then choose Lighting, Shadows from your Panel drop-down menu. Your graphics card will do the rest, and project hardware shadows from your lights, thus eliminating all the guesswork from shadow composition. Now swing your lights around in real time for the real fun. Just remember that more expensive cards will really come into play here.

HARD OR SOFT LIGHT

One of the primary tasks of a Director of Photography, aside from setting proper film exposure levels, is to define the feel and quality of the light, in order to reflect the emotional intentions of a script. The primary way this is done is to establish whether the light is seemingly soft or hard in its behavior. In CG terms, this relates to a sense of diffuse or specular light. For physical stage work, this can be controlled by gobos, cookies, scrims, and diffusers. You don't have the luxury of such devices, but certain Maya 6.0 tricks can mimic these qualities. The earlier tip "Cookies and Gobos" in this chapter describes ways to mimic a gobo light distribution, but these do little for a sense of softness. There are a number of ways to achieve soft qualities with normally all-specular CG lights: First, you can manipulate shadow maps; next, you can play with light decays, area lights, or light domes; last, you can use the correct simulation of true global illumination. GI can still be prohibitive, so let's look at standard CG lights. For basic softer shadows, shadow map resolution can be turned down, but there will be an innate loss of accuracy and aliasing. It is better to turn Dmap Filter Size to 3 or 4 in the Depth Map Shadow Attributes, but be ready for a hit in render time. This will also not establish a transition of hard to soft at a shadow's terminus, so use of an area light may be in order. Area lights are nothing more than a close-knit group of point lights, so the shadow implications are severe (see the tip "Fear of Point Light Shadow Maps" in this chapter). A great alternative to area lights are cubic arrays, explored in the tip "Cubic Point Arrays," also in this chapter. Next down the line is the use of light domes (see the tip "Poor Man's Global Illumination" in this chapter), which is usually a good solution to general soft illumination. For the brazen and bold, true raytraced GI using Mental Ray or the like is the most accurate and convincing, but nothing comes for free, especially GI, come render time.

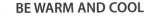

BE WARM AND COOL

This is one tip where we can learn from the boldest and simplest graphics in commercial art, comic books. Comic artists are limited in the range of color or tonal options they have to work from, so they rely on the oldest principle in art, that of warm/cool color opposition. This approach states that the key light should be warm in hue, while the shadows should go cool. This diametric opposition psychologically establishes a feeling of depth to an otherwise 2D image. The nice thing about applying this principle in CG is that you have lots of avenues in which to integrate it. The easiest is to add a yellow-orange hue into your primary key, and cool blue into your fill sources or shadow color. This is certainly something to always add to your scenes to some degree, but much more subtle ways of implementing this dynamic hue shift exist. To give your specular sheens much more life, map a basic 2D Fractal Map to the Specular Color in a shader's Attribute Editor. Turn the UV repeats down to 0.12, 0.12 for better scaling, and then turn the fractal Amplitude to somewhere around 0.4 to reduce contrast. Now open Color Balance and open the color editor for Color Gain. Put a saturated warm hue on it and a saturated cool hue on Color Offset. Now the specular highlight will maintain to white, but will transition into warm then cool, creating richly hued specular behavior when the object moves. Another area to implement warm/cool is in global illumination, where the HDR fill lighting sphere is held cool, while an added key light can be made warm.

CHEAPO FOG PARTICLES

Here is an age-old hack (er, highly advanced technique, that is) to add a sense of volume to underwater scenes. Underwater appearances require a strong sense of environmental fog with a fast dropoff, caustic light rays, and particulate matter to animate and convey a sense of current and movement. In regard to the latter, particles can be used to convey the particulates, but a much easier method uses foggy point lights. Start by establishing the basic environmental fog appearance and caustic light rays. Now drop in random point lights around and near the camera, switching off Illuminates By Default in its Attribute Editor. Put Decay Rate to Linear, and add Light Fog by pressing the checkered Texture Map button next to that field. Now edit the Fog Color to a blue-green similar to your environmental fog coloration and map a 2D Fractal Map to Density. Map a 2D Fractal to the Density in the Attribute Editor, and raise the Threshold to a value of 0.8 to 0.9. IPR render the scene to adjust quickly. There should now be a good simulation of discrete particles just from the randomness of the thresholded fractal noise. Complete the trick by gently animating a sway and bob to the point lights, then add fish and shipwrecks to suit.

⬤ ⬤ ⬤ DIRECTIONAL LIGHT SHADOW MAPPING

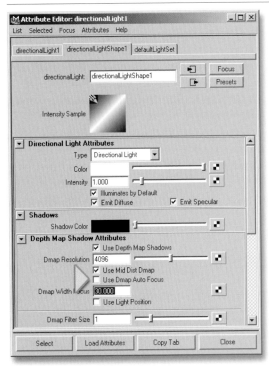

One of the advantages of directional lights is that they can cover vast areas of a scene very easily. One of the disadvantages is that they are a lousy way to cast a shadow map. They evaluate the full extent of the entire scene in order to calculate how to spread out the map across everything. The problem arises if you are modeling a cityscape of large worldspace; one shadow map pixel may take up the size of a building or car, even with an 8000 pixel resolution. Maya provides one way around this by unchecking Depth Map Auto-Focus in Depth Map Shadow Attributes. Now an angle of view can be input into the Depth Width Focus field in order to narrow down the spread of the width considerably and get more resolution where you need it. Note the check box for Use Light Position to help center the position of the map. Better yet, use Shadow Lights (tip of the same name in this chapter) to put shadows exactly where you want them, independent of key light position.

Rags to Rendering

GET A GRIP ON
SHADING

At the end of the day, it all comes down to the rendering. Character performance carries the emotion, but rendering carries the eye. As with lighting, it is an area in Maya where the talent and per-

Rags to Rendering

getting a grip on shading

sonality of the artist can shine through. However, many artists overlook the tremendous creative opportunities that Maya offers, relying on simplistic or downloaded shaders rather than understanding the true nature of building creative shader networks. Aside from being one of the better modeling packages on the market, Maya boasts one of the best creative environments for creating materials and shaders. Other renderers may be faster or less RAM-intensive, but the capability to quickly sculpt out a rich intended finish is a real strength of Maya. New features to version 6.0 like High Quality Hardware Shading or Photoshop integration allow very fast and efficient workflows. The node-based architecture inherent in the package carries over well into the shading environment, offering a rich array of connections and possible animated techniques. The recent addition of the Mental Ray renderer into the package further opens up the GI horizon for Maya artists. These rendering tips are gleaned from years of experience and will help you move from that flat shaded K-car of a rendering to a gleaming Lamborghini.

IMPERFECTION IS YOUR GOAL

Not a motto from some 12-step rehab program, rather this is a good way to consistently approach texturing and shading. Good CGI is imperfect CGI because the eye is very sensitive to repetition and consistency. Basic ways to provide inconsistencies are slightly randomizing modeling vertices (as discussed in Chapter 3, "The Glamorous World of Modeling: Work Smarter, Not Harder"); mapping fractal texturing to lighting (as discussed in the previous chapter, Chapter 4: "Embracing the Revolution: Lighting Your Way"); creating variations and grime in the texture map during painting; adding subtle random keyframes in your camera animation; and adding rich variations in the shaders themselves, such as randomness in specular, diffuse, displacement, and bump maps. The following image shows these principles applied. Every decision you make in the pipeline should be guided by this quest to be imperfect!

PROCEDURAL MAPPING VERSUS SCANNED FILES

The shading environment in Maya is very rich, and most of that depth is accessed from the tools offered under the Create Render Node menu initiated through the NASCAR flag button in a shader's Attribute Editor. A basic decision one must make under the Textures tab is whether to choose 2D or 3D textures. 2D textures generally are computed "slices of cheese," being either file textures from scanned imagery or procedural routines that only calculate a thin veneer of data. 3D textures are generally procedural solid "blocks of cheese," meaning that pure calculation is used to derive them instead of using predetermined texture maps to achieve a true volumetric representation. File textures generally consume few CPU cycles but lots of RAM, whereas procedural textures are the inverse. How you decide which to use depends on the nature of what you are trying to achieve, but if performance is a concern (when isn't it?), convert any calculation-heavy 3D texture to a speedy 2D file texture using Multilister, Edit, Convert to File Texture. For those preferring the Hypershade, use Hypershade, Edit, Convert to File Texture. The original 3D shader is discarded and reattached to a new shader with the 2D file substituted. Ah, the joys of automation.

MULTILISTER VERSUS HYPERSHADE—QUE ES MAS MACHO?

Maya always offers multiple ways to skin the cat, as the saying goes. One example is the interface options available to create shader networks. A holdover from the days of Alias PowerAnimator is the Multilister, a basic layout of shader, light, and camera nodes. In an effort to modernize, Maya has added the Hypershade panel to replace it, adding a snazzier name, more consolidation of tools, and a way to visually inspect connections between shader networks, not unlike the Hypergraph for geometry. Both accomplish the same end, so use the one appropriate to your preference or need. Functionally, the Hypershade has surpassed the Multilister, but the Multilister is preferred by the old guard because it's speedier and it provides a very direct way to inspect which nodes are connected to a particular network. The Hypershade is preferable for learning how connections are made, but it often tells more than is needed for basic connections. So, the Multilister is better for those who don't need the slowdown of graphic layouts of their networks, whereas the Hypershade is better for those who want to pick them apart or rearrange precise connections. Que es mas macho? That's up to you.

BAKING THE LIGHT

Though it sounds like an art film title, baking light is a handy way to speed up renders by converting lights into Incandescence maps. The downside of course is that there is no real lighting for characters to interact with, but for static background surfaces, it is a great optimizing method. However, remember that you are trading CPU cycles for RAM use as the light calculation becomes a map. To bake light, select the objects you want to bake onto, go to the Multilister and select the Shading Group assigned, and then go to Multilister, Edit, Convert to File Texture options. Check Bake Shading Group Lighting and Anti-Alias and choose an appropriate resolution. Note that shadows can also be baked in. Accept, and the geometry will be assigned to a new shader that has the lighting maps already attached. Note that it will create a Surface shader by default, so if more control is desired, create a new Blinn shader, connect these maps to the Incandescence channel, and turn Color to black.

COLOR OFFSET AND GAIN—THE KEY TO SHADER NETWORKS

Maya shader networks really open up when the Map button is exploited to create chains of operations in order to reach an end result. For instance, instead of looking at the Map selections as an end target selection, look at it as the beginning of a range of possible connections. A typical use of "Map Chaining" is to use the Color Gain and Color Offset map buttons under most texture node's Color Balance section to chain ramps or files in order to shape or sculpt a desired look. Much more than a simplistic level adjustment, Color Gain is a multiplier, enabling multiplication of one file by another. This can modify or erode a texture file, enabling multiple multiplication events that can form very useful looks. For instance, areas can be cut away from an image because a black region (for example, 0,0,0) is multiplied by the source pixel value (for example, 1,1,1), creating a black region in that area. This can be driven from any 2D or 3D Texture, but frequently Ramp Textures are used. Likewise, Color Offset, which is mathematically an add function, enables an addition of texture to an existing file. Creativity can really open up when successive and clever connections are made with these two strategies. For example, a brick wall can be made by first multiplying a Grid Texture onto the Alpha Gain of a Fractal Texture Bump map. Next, 2D Noise Textures can be added to the Grid Texture connected through the Grid's Alpha Gain to disturb the precise grid linework. Alpha Gain and Offset are used over color operators because Bump mapping is an 8-bit process and uses these for its calculations. Thinking of all connections as effective math operations can enable end results to be better understood and predicted. Generally, though, Color Gain acts as a subtractive device due to its multiplication, and Color Offset acts as an additive device. Shaping or modifying textures can lead to really fantastic results (especially animated), and you will enjoy the use of this knowledge for some time to come.

THE JOY OF RAMPS

Another great tool in your rendering arsenal is the Ramp Texture. Used for much more than color blends, the Ramp Texture is the true workhorse of the shader creation workflow. By capitalizing on the Ramp Texture's UV options, noise functions, and Color Gain/Offset chaining capabilities, this seemingly simple tool can be put to clever use. Also, the capability to pipe a texture node into each slider makes the Ramp Texture very powerful indeed. Make sure you understand and explore the excellent noise function made available in the Ramp Texture. The noise in the general Ramp Attributes section is for spatial distribution, whereas the HSV Color Noise section can enable the creation of very subtle variations, which are a great way to introduce imperfections into many aspects of your work. Trying out the various Ramp Texture distributions found in the Type pull-down menu can provide a basic array of geometric forms. Another great trick is to pipe a texture through the Ramp Texture using Color Gain to add noise or imperfections. With ingenuity, texture maps can be replaced with simple Ramp Textures, as the spaceman example above shows.

THE UNDERDOG OF SPECULAR MAPPING

Specularity is often overlooked as an important attribute in lieu of more developed color mapping or bumps. In fact, it is the key to true photorealism. A flat, consistent specular high-light rarely exists in the real world, so by perturbing your highlights with Specular mapping, you can get a more natural and convincing look for objects. It is also a key method for sepa-rating appearances of differing materials that have various specular behaviors. Study high-lights on objects around you and think of how you might map the effects. With metals, adding color and variance to the specular look is essential. Start by using a 2D Fractal Texture mapped to the Specular Color on a Blinn shader. Next, change the UV repeats of the fractal down to 0.2 and 0.2 to create a broader wash, lower the Fractal Amplitude to reduce contrast, and then add a warm hue into the Color Gain and a cool hue into the Color Offset. This will create a color shift into the specular, giving a slight iridescence as the camera moves. With proper adjustment, your surfaces will become much more photorealistic and richer in behavior as the camera moves over them.

HEAVY METAL RENDERING

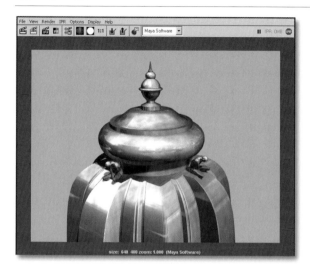

CG metallic surfaces can range from banal flying logos to lustrous, beat-up, heat-distressed jet engines. Metals can be done poorly without some guidelines, but they are pretty easy to achieve with the proper setup. Start with a Blinn shading model, reduce Diffuse (essential to metal), reduce Specular Rolloff, increase Eccentricity, use a high-frequency (UV repeats of 1000) noise bump map (very small bump value), and add a fractal specular map with warm and cool Color Gain and Offset as described in the previous tip. Map the Color Offset with a noisy hue Ramp Texture to add heat-distressed iridescence. This solution works well for weathered and corroded metals. For shiny new aluminum or chrome, use a good reflection map. With a bit of noodling in IPR, you should start to feel the metal getting heavy right in front of you.

   GREEN SCREEN PLAYBLASTING

Playblast is the staple diet of judging animation in Maya. It provides a quick hardware capture of successive frames in order to evaluate your animation moves in real time. In most cases it works fine, but a problem exists if you ever need an alpha channel to do a slap comp over live action or composite separate pieces of a model together. Because Playblast does not offer any alpha channel, a simple workaround is to create your own green screen there by changing the background color to green in Window, Settings/Preferences, Colors. Then do a simple chroma key in your compositing package. Because there is typically no anti-aliasing in Playblast output, alpha can be cleanly and neatly extracted. Simple but useful.

EMBRACING DIRT AND GRIME

Dirt and grime are not only an unavoidable part of life (especially with kids), but they are actually *encouraged* in CG rendering. A common method is to dirty up your texture maps, but an easier and more spatially coherent method is to use 3D procedural methods in Maya's shader networks. Create a basic Lambert shader with a dark black color and then use a 3D Solid Fractal Texture as a transparency map. Use this shader as an overlay to any other base shader underlay in a Layered shader. Adjust the Ripples of the 3D Fractal Texture to 1.0, 0.1, 0.1 to get the proper vertical streaking and density. Use of a grayscale Ramp Texture on the Color Offset can taper it down to create drip marks. Age can be accelerated by using a subtle noisy hue Ramp Texture mapped to the Color Offset of the color map to discolor and slightly yellow the object. Color Remap can be used to further alter the original color spectrum. Erosion can be made on the bump map with a Color Remap as well, altering and intensifying the bump map. Rust and iridescent oil can be created by color mapping a noisy hue Ramp Texture on top of the rest using another layer in the shader. The beauty of using solid procedurals in all this is that they will not display UV mapping artifacts and will scale properly in distance. Who knew you would grow to love dirt this much?

TRIPLANAR PROJECTION TO THE RESCUE

Projection maps are the mainstay of environmental surfaces for a few reasons. First, wall surfaces need continuity with each other because brick coursings and trim lines need to match wall to wall. Projections offer a worldspace solution to this problem. The problem arises when one needs to map irregular walls, perhaps at odd angles to each other. We all know of the basic planar or cylindrical projection. Triplanar projection is one of a few lesser-known projection types Maya offers that is highly useful for architecture. Triplanar should not be confused with common box or cubic projection, which emanates all projections from the center outward on six planar faces. Triplanar is similar to planar, but it offers three axes of projection, one of which is chosen by the normal of the surface. As long as a surface face is within 45 degrees of a given projection face, it will pick up that respective face. Clearly, this is not a projection type for curving or organic models, but for orthographic architectural forms, it is the magic bullet because all walls can be mapped in one fell swoop with one shader. The examples shown of the boiler room and stone temple were done with nearly one shader, with no messy UVs to clean up!

LAYER IT ON

3D rendering is typically performed in one pass, which is known as rendering "in camera." For small projects or solo work, this is fine, but on large feature film projects where there are multiple chefs in the kitchen, this can be problematic. No one wants to re-render umpteen hours for a minute color change in your CG character's shoelaces. So rendering by layers or passes is commonly done, breaking one image into passes such as diffuse, specular, reflection, shadow, occlusion, HDR, z-depth, volumetric, matte, and so on, and combining them in a compositing package for fine control. This grouping may also be multiplied again by breaking elements up into foreground, mid-ground, and background to enable easier matting or perhaps to handle an otherwise massive render load. Luckily, Maya has accommodated this workflow by establishing Render Layers and Passes. Render Layers are created in the Layer Editor and used to isolate elements during a render. Render Passes are used to render the passes separately and can be found by highlighting a Render Layer in the Layer Editor and then choosing Layers, Layer Attributes. The Render Pass Options list the various choices. These can also be found in Render Globals, Maya Software, Render Layer/Pass Control by choosing Enable Render Layer or Passes. Note that you must Batch Render to enable any of this, and even though the Render Layer controls reside on the Maya Software panel, it controls Mental Ray output as well.

PASS THAT SHADOW PLEASE

Even though the previous tip may be more trouble to set up than you might want to deal with, a separate shadow pass is frequently useful for standard rendering, as the capability to blur shadows or composite them separately over live action backgrounds is always useful. Various methods can be employed to achieve this, but here are a few: First, the Render Passes control mentioned previously works well, but it creates the shadow in the alpha channel. Next, clever use of a shader's Matte Opacity can give matting results that can leave shadows on white surfaces. Lastly, the Use Background shader is very useful for shadow passes when the background is set to white and the shader is assigned to all surfaces. This same shader is useful for simple composites where the live action background plate is set up as an animated image plane and receives shadows from objects reconstructed from and matching the plate.

STRIKING A CHORD LENGTH

UV texturing is now replacing NURBS parameterized texturing because polygons are once again in vogue. One benefit of UV texturing is the texture can be totally unrelated to surface idiosyncrasies (although at a high labor cost in manually setting it all up). If you choose to take the easier road, texturing with NURBS, you may find stretching of the texture from the varying parameterization of the modeling. An easy fix for this is to select the object, and then in the Attribute Editor under Texture Map, choose Fix Texture Warp. This will spread the map evenly according to chord length, resulting in a consistent mapping.

   GLOW FLICKERING NO MORE

Nothing is more annoying than investing hours of rendering and having your shader glow flicker like there is an ensuing California power brownout in your scene. There are a few fixes for this, however. First, render a still frame with satisfactory glow settings in the Render View, and then in the Attribute Editor of the Multilister shaderGlow, disable Auto Exposure. Now look at your separate Maya Output window and put the Glow and Halo Intensity Normalization Factors values into the Glow and Halo Intensity fields. If any flickering continues on very small objects, select the geometry and, in the Attribute Editor, increase the Shading Samples under Render Stats. If only California had it this easy.

DETERMINING TEXTURE RESOLUTION

A dilemma has existed through the ages about which texture resolution is proper for a project. Answers have been invoked from Ouiji boards and Magic 8 balls, but the solution is really quite simple. 3D rendering is effectively all matrix calculation, where the color of a pixel is determined from the relation of various spaces, such as object or screen space. A texture map should ideally match the screen space of what it occupies in the render, but animation and perspective alter that simplicity. A good rule of thumb is to find the nearest proximity of the texture in relation to screen resolution and then scale down the resolution 75 percent. Texture aliasing should be avoided like mad cows, so shooting a bit smaller than screen resolution will ensure some stability in the texture, which will get visually crisper in animation anyway. Also, smaller textures equal less RAM and shorter render times, which equal happier producers and clients—who knew texture resolution could ultimately lead to world peace?

SAMPLER INFO FACING RATIO MANIA

This rather clunky-sounding term can bring your shaders up more than a few notches. Facing Ratio is a method of deriving values on a surface as the normal faces or swings away from camera. This value can be used for example for increasing reflection as a window rotates away from camera (known as the fresnel effect). Creating rim lighting, transparent ghost-like edges, or X-ray glow effects are other common uses depending on what channel Facing Ratio is applied to. To use it, create a Utility Node called Sampler Info in the Work Area in the Hypershade panel. Next, create a Ramp Texture and delete the place2dTexture icon. Now MMB drag the Sampler Info over the Ramp and choose Other to bring up the Connection Editor. Pick Facing Ratio in the left column and connect to Uv Coord, V Coord in the right column. Now MMB drag the Ramp Texture onto the attribute of choice in your shader. Change the Ramp Texture to grayscale and IPR render in the Render View. Next, alter the Ramp Texture distribution to good effect. Now use the Creative Ingenuity button and apply throughout your project.

RENDER SCRIPTS RULE!

```
C:\WINNT\System32\cmd.exe                                    _|□|×|
C:\>Render -help
Usage: Render <options> <filename>
      where <filename> is a Maya ASCII or a Maya Binary file.

startFrame          -s  <float>    starting frame for an animation sequence
endFrame            -e  <float>    end frame for an animation sequence
byFrame             -b  <float>    by frame (or step)
                                   for an animation sequence
startExtension      -se <int>      starting number for the output image
                                   frame file name extensions
byExtension         -be <int>      by extension (or step) for the output
                                   image frame file name extension
extensionPadding    -pad <int>     number of digits in the output image
                                   frame file name extension

project             -proj <dir>    project directory to use
renderDirectory     -rd  <path>    directory in which to store image file

image               -im <filename> image file output name (identical to -p)
pix                 -p  <filename> image file output name (identical to -im)

mayaExtension       -me <boolean>  append maya file name to image name
                                   if true
mayaFormat          -mf <boolean>  append image file format to image name
                                   if true

cameraOverride      -cam <name>    all subsequent -im -p -ar -sa flags
                                   apply only to <camera_name>
```

Most Maya users are taught to use the Render View for still render evaluation and Batch Rendering for animations. A much better way to render strings of frames is from the command line render. Open a DOS shell by going to Windows Start, Run and typing `cmd`. Look at your command line options and flags by typing `Render -h`. This will return back a flood of usage descriptions. Next, open Notepad and type a string following `Render <options> <your_scenefile.mb>`. Commonly used flags are `-s start_frame`, `-e end_frame`, `-b by_frame`, `-p output_file_prefix`, `-cam camera_name`, `-x X_resolution`, `-y Y_resolution`, `-of output_format`, `-pad padding_digits`, and `-n number_of_processors`. Note that there are also commands not found in the Render Global GUI such as `xLeft`, `xRight`, `yLeft`, and `yRight` for rendering sub-regions. An example might be as follows: `Render -s 1 -e 10 -b 1 -p Foo -cam persp -pad 4 -n 2 -x 720 -y 486 -of tif my_scenefile.mb`. This would render Foo.0001-10.tif. The advantage here is that you can shut down the Maya session to take full advantage of RAM and CPU cycles. If you want a record of the session to check RAM load, render times, and so on, you can pipe the output verbiage into a file by appending `> outfile.txt` after the render command in the text file. Lastly, suffix your text file with `.bat` to create an executable file and double-click when you're ready to rumble.

LAYERED SHADERS TO GO

Perhaps the biggest workhorse of all shader models is the Layered shader. It is in fact not a shading model at all but is a very handy method of ascribing multiple shading models to a single surface. More than just a way to lay dirt or decals over a base surface, it can be used to create very complex shaders by mixing various shading models, such as Anisotropic, Lambert, and a Ramp shader all on one surface together. It is conceptually an "onion skin" of shaders piled on top of each other, with respective Transparency attributes revealing each in succession. To create a Layered shader, first create the shaders you want to layer. Next create a Layered shader and MMB-drag each of your component shaders alongside the default green base. After you have brought them all in, you can delete the default layer and rearrange the layers as you like by MMB-dragging them into a new order. The uppermost of the stacked onion skin will be at the far left. It is helpful to name each shader with a descriptive name to avoid confusion. Now render in IPR and modify each layer's transparencies with holdout maps to create a work of art (hopefully). Standard uses for Layered shaders are for rust or barnacle buildup, oil stains, billboards on a wall, and so on, but the sky is truly the limit as always in 3D. One drawback to Layered shaders, however, is that they will only use one displacement map if each shader has one assigned.

TO PREMULT OR NOT TO PREMULT

Premultiplication of alpha is one of those topics that causes endless confusion for many Maya artists. Premult essentially deals with how Maya decides to anti-alias edges against a background without knowing what the background really is. Maya premultiplies the RGB images against a black background according to the alpha that is generated by the object. This means that there is a slight black fringe of anti-aliased pixels surrounding every object because it can only average the edge against a black background. If Maya knew what the background plate was at the time of rendering, it could accurately create the anti-aliasing of the alpha, but without it, all it can do is anti-alias against black. This does not pose a problem if your compositing package expects a premultiplied image, but some do not, and thus a black halo appears around the objects. Shake and After Effects give you the option to un-premult the image during import, which can also alleviate the problem. Maya by default has Premultiplication turned on, but it is accessible in Render Globals, Maya Software, Render Options, Color/Compositing, Premultiply. If turned off, Premultiply Threshold allows a variable amount primarily for gaming work. In general, you should leave it on, but check with your friendly neighborhood compositor before committing an overnight render.

GETTING WET

Water tends to be one of the harder elements to faithfully re-create in CG. Behavior-wise, Maya Fluids begins to offer a solution for this slippery problem (sorry). But if you simply need to show a surface that appears wet or a good car-paint appearance, there is an easy setup using Blinn shader attributes. In this shader, there is Specular Rolloff, which most tend to think only affects specular highlights. In fact, this attribute also affects reflection maps and raytraced reflection, the essential components of wet appearances. Specular Rolloff pushes the specular and reflection out to the edges away from camera normal, giving the appearance of wet edges. Raise the value from default .2 to around 3 or 4 and lower the Eccentricity down to .2 or so. You may need to raise the Specular Color to a value higher than 1 as well, perhaps 3 or 4. Lastly, remember that reflectivity should generally be no more than 1/Specular Color, so with a value of 4, the reflectivity should be set at .25.

COLOR REMAPPING

Color Remapping is a great command that many pass up on their road to rendering. Color Remap is primarily used for replacing a texture's tonal range with one from another file's for surreal or abstract effects. For example, green alien skin can be made by remapping a facial skin tone map with lizard skin. The hue and value of the original file are remapped to a color ramp with hue assigned to U and value to V. The original color hue is lost as it connects to a V ramp, but new color values or textures can be substituted. Start with an image assigned to a File Texture, and then in its Attribute Editor, choose Effects, Insert Color Remap. A Ramp Texture is then displayed, altering the color of the original texture. Reduce the ramp to a black-to-white grayscale and observe that the tonal range is alterable, similar to the curves function in Photoshop. Now add multiple sliders with various hues or textures mapped to them, and the fun begins. This is a great way to age, alter, or discolor existing maps or create a little psychedelia along the way.

A HEAD OF THE GAME

Modeling a human head is already difficult in itself, but on top of that comes the tedious UV unwrapping process. After you have your model complete and are ready to move on to unwrapping UVs, try this precious trick. Make a duplicate of your head model, and then apply Polygons, Average Vertices. Apply this multiple times until your model no longer has major undercut regions around the areas of the nose, lips, eyes, and ears. Next, apply a cylindrical UV coordinate projection with a simple grid texture. Tile it a few times so you can see how the UVs are mapping onto your model. The next step is to transfer just the UVs onto the original head model by selecting Polygons, Transfer, UV Sets.

RETURN TO NORMALCY

Deadlines are often tight and challenging to meet, with little room for mistakes. Probably the most common mistake made in polygonal modeling is inverted normals. This can inadvertantly result from many operations like mirroring an object, creating a polygon in the wrong direction, or converting NURBS to polygons. A sure way to know if objects in your scene have inverted normals is to uncheck the Lighting, Two Sided Lighting option in your viewport panel drop-down menu. Now any objects that appear black in your scene have inverted normals and require some quick attention through Edit Polygons, Normals, Reverse.

SHADING GROUP SELECTION TOOL

Trying to manage a large number of shaders using the Multilister can be confusing when trying to remember what objects are attached to what shaders. On the far left column in the Multilister interface, you will find a series of icons that are very useful in this regard. The first icon in that column is the Shading Group Selection tool. If this tool is selected, your standard selection cursor icon will change. Select a shader from within the Multilister and it will highlight in blue, with all objects in your scene that are attached to that shader selected. After you're done, be sure to switch back to your regular selection tool by pressing any of the QWERTY keys, because the flip side of this tool is that it will also assign the highlighted material to any object you select while active.

FADE INTO THE BACKGROUND

Often you need to cast interactive shadows of a CG object onto a live-action background (known as a "plate"). It is a trivial affair to do the compositing once a shadow pass is generated, but not so trivial to have the shadow match and rake across the forms in the plate. There is a magic bullet for just this need in Rendering Menu, Lighting/Shading, Assign New Material, Use Background. Start by loading a backgound image as an Image Plane and modeling the basic forms against it as required to receive the shadows. Now attach their geometry to the Use Background shader. Acting conceptually like a chameleon's skin, the objects inherit the background's color without calculating any specularity or lighting characteristics. Now when shadows are turned on in your lighting rig, the shader will receive the shadows, effectively compositing the shadows directly onto the plate. Either render the backgound directly out of Maya or render a separate shadow pass for compositing (see the "Pass that Shadow Please" tip in this chapter). Note that the live-action forms that were modeled can now cast shadows onto the CG object for full CG integration nirvana.

HIGH QUALITY SHADING

Lighting a 3D scene doesn't need to be the frustrating task we all know it can be at times. We spend a lot of time and energy setting up the lights and shadows appropriately while making sure the material settings are working well in the scene. New in version 6.0, High Quality Shading can greatly help minimize the iterative guesswork when lighting a scene. High Quality Shading turns your viewport into a hardware-driven, real-time interactive render window by displaying accurate light and shadow information as well as accurate specular highlights and material settings such as bump maps and transparencies. Ray tracing is not yet supported in High Quality Shading, so don't expect to see reflections. To enable High Quality Shading, navigate to the shading pull-down menu in the viewport under Shading, High Quality Rendering. Be sure to have Shadows selected under the lighting pull-down menu in the viewport as well. Just remember that more expensive cards will really come into play here.

TEST TEXTURES

Make texture maps or even animated textures with Test Texture, a new feature in version 6.0. It's difficult when working with procedural textures and having only a thumbnail image to view it with because details are lost or near impossible to read. With Test Texture, the texture can be viewed in the render view window at any resolution, and animated textures can even be saved as a sequence of images that can later be brought back and used as an animation. Test Texture is accessed in the Hypershade window found under Windows, Rendering Editors, Hypershade. Once you're in Hypershade, select the texture node (it won't work on the material group level), then RMB, Test Texture, or navigate to Edit, Test Texture in the Hypershade window.

RGB LIGHTING PASSES

Here is a pretty cool trick used by effects animation pros to light their particles or volumetrics. Effects animation tends to be fairly unpleasant to re-render, as particle run-ups and render times can be huge. Add a hard-to-please art director or supervisor, and the need for lighting in post arises. Because particle rendering tends to be semi-monotonous in hue but rich in value, essentially grayscale renders can be placed in each channel of an RGB render, allowing a tweak of fill and key values in compositing rather than rendering. Start by software rendering a particle cloud, but place three lights in different quadrants around the cloud. Color each light as a primary red, green, and blue. Render the sequence, and then in compositing, import three copies of the file. On one, copy the red channel to the other blue and green slots. On the other two, do the same with the blue and green channels. Then set up an add-mix of the three so that varying adds of each can establish key or fill ratios, which can be easily changed based on the add amount of each channel.

PHOTOSHOP AND MAYA GET MARRIED

One of the most significant new features in version 6.0 is the ability to streamline the texturing process by truly integrating with Photoshop. Photoshop Document (PSD) textures are now fully supported not only as a file format but also with full automation of relating layer sets in the Photoshop file to channel connections in a sample shader. Start by selecting a poly object, and then choose Texturing, Created PSD Texture in the Rendering menu. A dialog will appear with options such as resolution, optional automatic UV snapshot (sweet!), and a selection of which shader attributes will end up as a layer set in the PSD file. Choose Create and the file creates, but most conveniently all shader connections are made as well. Have fun in your texturing, save the PSD file, and then choose Texturing, Update PSD Textures to update your model. Features like these really help take out the inherent tediousness of CG and keep our eyes on the prize, the rendering itself.

From
Home Movies
to Hollywood

*Lights, action, and CG camera!
Camerawork is another one of those
areas in which, without a little care
and affection, your work will unfortunately*

From Home Movies to Hollywood

camerawork basics

*fall quite flat. Good camerawork, like charac-
ter animation, is a lifelong study, offering
much depth and range for what can be
learned and accomplished. In Hollywood, the
masters of camerawork are termed DPs, or
Directors of Photography. The art of cinema
that they have perfected is clearly the place to
begin to glean inspiration and technique. CG
camerawork, however, is odd in that it is not
bound to the physical world, and as such, it
has few of the imperfections and anomalies
that gravity and mechanics tend to leave as
signatures on Hollywood films. Much like
adding synthetic film grain and lens flares on
otherwise pristine CG imagery, we need that
imperfection to really have our brain feel that
the work is real and valid. As we accustom
ourselves to the precision of the digital aes-
thetic, perhaps this will fade, but for now
great attention should be paid to what the
legendary DPs have skillfully forged prior
to CG.*

RULE OF THIRDS

The first step in good camerawork is creating the composition of the image. You may be starting from storyboards where the basic layout is worked out already, or you may be creating and visualizing each shot directly in 3D. Whatever the case, the eye of the camera needs to be carefully considered by trying to establish a psychologically motivated point of view and dynamic tension of elements. Possibly the worst strategy is to dead center your subject, but there are DPs who can make even that succeed. It's better to reinforce a sense of depth of the 2D image by dividing up the screen into vertical thirds and placing a near-ground object centered on one dividing line and a distant object on the other. This will establish field of view and dynamic tension with little effort. Of course good composition consists of much more than that and should weigh in factors such as emotion, color relationships, negative and positive space, tone, key, and narrative. Overall, good composition is pleasing, stimulating, or confounding and always leads the eye directly and gracefully to where the director intends.

PERSPECTIVE BASICS

One of the ironies of computer graphics is that without prior training in the arts or design, many CG artists are never exposed to the principles of perspective because our software effortlessly calculates it in real time. Perspective is always considered the starting point for all artwork except in CG. Granted, many 3D artists acquire an innate feel for space and composition, but evidence of a lack of sensitivity to perspective abounds in the field. Developing a simple sensitivity to perspective is useful in arriving at a good composition, and it also shows a refined eye. The study of perspective is the analysis of vanishing points and how they fall within a frame. One-point perspective is simply a level camera with a single vanishing point at the center, usually in frame. Symmetrical and rigid in nature, it is usually best to avoid it. Two-point perspective is the most widely used by architectural delineators and photographers, as it introduces two vanishing points off either side of the image and maintains straight vertical lines. Three-point perspective allows full freedom of vanishing points, with two off either side and a third running up or down from the image. 3D packages operate in this mode naturally, but two point and single point can be achieved with proper camera orientation. A basic assumption is that if people's heads are aligned with the horizon line, it infers that the camera is at eye height above the ground. The next tip shows how Maya can be tricked into skewing the principles of perspective.

PERCEPTUAL PERSPECTIVE CORRECTION

A long-standing technique preferred by architectural illustrators and large-format photographers is to eliminate the third vanishing point while maintaining the position of the horizon line and key features. This amounts to effectively straightening out the converging vertical lines a camera would see as it tilts skyward. While looking upward at a very tall structure such as a skyscraper, this phenomenon is unavoidable, but with lower structures, or even in a room, your brain compensates for the optical taper, keeping verticals parallel and delivering a perceptually correct view. You can test this out simply by tilting your head up toward the ceiling as you watch a corner of a room. Now do the same thing with a camera and observe the effect. Although the tapering is optically correct, being able to eliminate it in a 2D image such as a photograph or CG render creates a much more pleasing and refined look. Maya luckily has included the virtual analog of a perspective shift lens in a commonly overlooked attribute in the Camera Attribute Editor called Film Offset. Of little use in animated cameras (except for excellent abstraction potential), it shifts the virtual film plane in screen space x or y a given amount. To start, position a camera near the bottom of a tall building-shaped cube. Use the local camera command Panel View, Camera Tools, Yaw-Pitch Tool to then tilt upward, setting the horizon line at a given position. Next, under the Camera Attribute Editor, Film Back, Film Offset, type an arbitrary number such as .3 in the second field (y). The horizon will shift down below frame, but raise it back up to the same level with the Yaw-Pitch Tool. Now you will have the same view but with parallel vertical edges. If it is not yet parallel, try increasing or decreasing the Film Offset value and Yaw-Pitch accordingly. Your still renders can now look much more refined with this great technique. For something really wild, increase your field of view to a very large value and add Film Offset to both x and y. Now tumble the camera through your own version of Hitchcock's *Vertigo*!

PANEL VIEW VERSUS FILM BACK VERSUS RESOLUTION

Alias PowerAnimator, the original source for much of what is good in Maya, was one of the first packages to relate real-world optics and film properties to the virtual world of 3D cameras. Dubbed the Optical Toolkit back then, those functions now reside in Maya's Camera Attribute Editor. It basically consists of letting the user define a known film format around which to structure the 3D rendering, in effect placing film into the package. This makes integration with film or video immensely easier during compositing, but it does cause some confusion when relating the multiple viewing frames that a render can be interpreted through in Maya. First, go to Camera Attribute Editor, Film Back, Film Gate, and decide on an aspect ratio and format to work with, say 35mm 1.85 Projection. This will change your focal length (field of view), so enter, say, 63 in Camera Attributes, Angle of View. You still will not see the 1.85 letterbox aspect ratio in the viewing panel, so next you must apply a viewing gate there with Panel View, Camera Settings, Film Gate. Now a proper gate is visible, illustrating that the panel view is quite arbitrary but can hold a proper gating. If you want to enlarge the image and reduce the space around it, type 1.05 in Camera Attribute Editor, Film Back, Overscan. This function enables viewing of animation in and out of frame. Next, type the same aspect ratio resolution in Render Globals and now try Panel View, Camera Settings, Resolution Gate. It should show the same gating, indicating that you are all on the same page, from viewing panel to film back to output resolution.

CREATING NATURAL CAMERA MOTION

Real-world camerawork has progressed from very static and slow movement to rapid cut, freeform handheld Steadicam-type movements. They both are shot with the aid of a human hand, and thus they have a distinctive, somewhat erratic signature. Perfectly interpolated CG camera moves will always look artificial because we are accustomed to the imperfections of real cameras. A good way to create these inconsistencies and aberrations is to use a randomizer MEL script (randKey.mel is a favorite found on Highend3d.com) or manually set random imperfections to create small jitters and shakes in the camera action. Simply insert a selection of random keyframes on an already-established camera curve and then slightly randomize them to alter its perfection. If done subtly, a much more natural motion can be achieved, and the difference will be amazing—one camera movement feels human and one mechanical.

PROFESSIONAL CAMERA ANIMATION SETUP

Most casual Maya users animate the lower nodes of the camera grouping. This is the most expedient way to animate a camera, but a more robust and professional method is to use multiple nodes to hold animation channels. Start by creating a three-node camera with Create, Cameras, Camera, Aim, and Up. Open the Outliner window and group the upper node three times, then rename each node, starting with the upper, as XYZ_Translate, then the next one down as Pan or Yrot (if Y up is used), next down as Tilt or Xrot, and next down as Roll or Zrot. Note the sequence of rotation is YXZ, not XYZ, preventing gimbal lock. Next, select the camera with Panel View, Select Camera and lock all the channels in the Channel Box. This will prevent any camera tumbling or movement that could ruin the setup because the lower node must stay untransformed. Then begin the process of keyframing the camera's motions by translating or rotating the appropriate node in the chain. Remember to only set a key for the respective channel in each node, so you may elect to lock out all channels but the one to be keyed. This lengthy setup achieves an easily editable, channel-independent mode of camera control. If a slight increase in roll is desired, it is easily set and doesn't affect any other channels as a single node camera animation would, which is a great advantage in tweaking a move. Lastly, channels are well-organized in this fashion for easy import and export of curve data to other packages, motion control rigs, and so on. After learning this method, people rarely go back!

CAMERA PROJECTION MAGIC

A major shift has occurred in the landscape (pardon the pun) of matte painting with the advent of 3D. Historically, complex background scenes that were prohibitively difficult to build used to be painted on glass, or more recently created in Photoshop, but are now projected into simple 3D layouts, enabling dimensional camera moves within the static painting. The technique used is that of camera projection, or using a perspective camera to project texturing information. Maya offers it as Perspective Projection, a projection type alongside the other standard types in the projection node, but it does require a bit of careful setup to succeed. Camera projection is useful to more than matte painters because it is an excellent way to reduce the weight of a heavily detailed model down to something that can be more easily painted. Tasks requiring the texturing of a huge number of parts can also be well-suited to this technique. Start with a collection of primitives and animate a camera pushing in, naming the camera Anim_Cam. Now study the parallax of the move and locate a point that maximizes the coverage of visible texture area. Copy the camera at that frame, strip out the animation, and name that camera Proj_Cam. Render a high-resolution 2k or 4k frame from Proj_Cam as a base for painting and then paint a color key over the various objects, assigning this file as a Perspective Projection map in a new shader's Incandescence channel. Assign all geometry to the shader and Choose Proj_Cam as the projecting camera under Camera Projection Attributes, Link To Camera. Now render a frame and check that the painting matches tightly to the geometry. If not, verify that the film back dimensions match the aspect ratio of the painting file. As the camera is now rendered throughout the sequence, you might find that this single projection may not be enough to properly texture all the surfaces that are revealed during the camera move. Surfaces that were partially behind other objects may display portions of the texture from the object in front. If this is the case, a second camera projection map for the occluded surfaces will be necessary, using alpha stenciling to paint in only what is necessary. This method is also excellent for dimensionalizing photography or 2D artwork. With a bit of practice, this is one of the great Killer Tips for Maya, so camera project on!

NO AUTO ANYTHING (ESPECIALLY CAMERA CLIPPING)

Automation is wonderful for such things as ATMs or the manufacturing of Twinkies. It is not so great when the success of your render depends on it. Maya includes an option called Auto Render Clip Plane in the Camera Attribute Editor that sounds like a good idea, but it can lead to indigestion and heartburn. It attempts to bind the clipping of the camera to the largest extent of the modeling, but because extreme clipping ranges are the number-one source of render problems, it is wise to uncheck it and set clipping manually. It only takes a minute, and your happiness following a night's render may depend on it. For that matter, Auto-anything in Maya can lead to problems and is best avoided. Remember not to exceed the ratio of near clip at 0.1 and far clip at 20,000 because the math gets fuzzy, and your render is susceptible to artifacts. Pushing up the ratio a decimal place to 1 and 200,000 can be a fine strategy if a higher far clip is needed, or worst case, the scene can be scaled down.

SIMPLIFY, SIMPLIFY FOR ANIMATION

Thoreau must have foreseen computer graphics back in his day, because if there is anything that is NOT simple, it is CG. Fighting back complexity is the name of the game in 3D, and one of the areas that suffers from too much of it is camera animation. If there is too much density, resolution, or geometry in your scene, animating a camera can be unresponsive and difficult. Try these handy tips to fight the madness and get control of your camera. Start with the Panel, Show pull-down, and turn off unnecessary elements in the scenes such as deformers or CVs. In the same menu is Isolate Select, which enables temporary hiding of unselected objects, along with bookmarks. Next, turn on Display, Fast Interaction. This command draws objects in lesser resolution as they fall away from camera, speeding up responsiveness. Next, try wireframe versus shaded display mode, using the "1" display option for NURBS. Also try Window, Settings/Preferences, Performance Settings to disable any expensive deformation calculations during playback. Lastly, there is the old standby of turning objects to bounding boxes via Display, Object Display, Bounding Box. What worked in the 80s still works today!

UNDOS THE VIEWS

Often when doing camera animation, you create a view and later want to return to it. Rather than try to relocate the camera, there are handy keyboard hotkeys just for this—the bracket keys, [and]. One undos and the other redos the preceding views (just like a Seussian tongue twister). That is how we do our undos and redos of our views, sir.

FILM FORMATS FOR NEWBIES

Film formats are a bit of a misnomer in CG because we don't really use film, but if you plan on doing feature film CG work, they are an inescapable fact of life. We adapt to the film world and not vice-versa, so Maya has a very convenient way to emulate film in the Film Gate settings in the Camera Attribute Editor.

The earlier tip, "Panel View Versus Film Back Versus Resolution," discusses how to set up the types listed, but these may be green to some who are new to the film world. Most theatrical releases are projected at a 1.85-to-1 aspect ratio, but that doesn't always mean they were shot that way. Also, a 2.28-to-1 aspect ratio is popular for epic widescreen features that might use a squeezing of the image as it is shot onto film that is unsqueezed at projection time, called an Anamorphic technique. Thus, Maya offers these various choices that a DP may make, which ripple down to the 3D visual effects artist. In the Film Gate options, 16mm choices are given but are rarely used. The common ones are the 35mm, especially 35mm Academy and 35mm 1.85 Projection. Academy is set at 1.33 to 1 and utilizes more of the celluloid area listed in the Camera Aperture fields in inches, but it is gated down in the theatre to a 1.85 crop. 35mm 1.85 Projection is useful when gating was used during shooting. The 35mm Anamorphic option is half of the 2.36 aspect ratio at 1.18 to 1, but it applies a Lens Squeeze ratio, resulting in thin vertical pixels. It is best avoided unless required for a show. 70mm Projection is commonly a 2.28-to-1 aspect ratio, and it creates a larger cinematic grandeur. VistaVision is next offered at a 1.5-to-1 aspect ratio with larger film back dimensions being 2 to 3 times the area of Academy. It is still commonly shot for visual effects plates. For the truly resolution-hungry, Maya includes Imax at a 1.34 aspect ratio and a whopping 2.7" × 2" area. Note the related resolutions for these sizes are set in Render Globals independently. Remember to set the proper lens Field of View as you change these because they alter the Focal Length.

ANIMATED IMAGE PLANES GONE WILD

A handy use for image planes beyond that of modeling tools is to use them as rough compositors, adding the live-action background as a sequence to view your CG objects over or match elements to. The trick is to keyframe the extension of the file sequence and relate it to your timeline so that frames load in tandem with the CG animation. Begin by adding the first frame as an image plane and fit to your chosen film back or resolution settings. Now, under the Image Plane Attributes, check Use Frame Extension. You will note that moving the time slider makes no change, so we need to keyframe the extension into a curve. Set the slider to frame 1 and right mouse button on the Frame Extension field to Set Key. Now go to your end frame of the Image Plane sequence, enter that number in the Frame Extension field, and Set Key again. Now the time slider should update the background. Using the Select button at the bottom of the Attribute Editor will load this curve in the Graph Editor, where you can double the rate, cycle or oscillate the playback, and so on by manipulating the curve and resultant mapping of extension values to time.

WRESTING CONTROL OF FCHECK

Fcheck has had a GUI front-end for a while now, but to really wrest control of it, try running it from the command line. Open a DOS shell and type `fcheck -h`, then get ready for a lot of text return. You will find a veritable treasure trove of controls made available, massive amounts more than in the watered-down GUI. You might even locate the name of its creator at the end, Arnaud Hervas. The most commonly used flags are `-n start end by`, `-s scale factor`, `-m zoom factor`, and `-r frame rate`. With just those options alone, you can look at 2k images scaled down by 3 but zoomed back up twice playing on twos in order to fit into your available RAM. There are also controls to change gamma or color space and even write out a sequence in a new format. Hunt around the options and realize it is a terrific Swiss Army knife of RAM players.

 ## IMAGE PLANE SPEEDUP

Maya can be run with garden-variety gaming graphics cards or expensive full-blown pixel-crunching workstation cards. A lot of work can be done with the inexpensive gaming cards, but there are a few areas in which they come up short: performance of image planes and hardware plane functions such as Artisan and PaintFX. Hardware plane issues demand the better cards, but here is an easy fix for image plane slowdowns occurring from changes in Color Gain or Alpha settings of the image plane. You will need to add this line to your Maya.env file located in your Maya folder in the Documents and Settings folder on your drive: `setenv MAYA_SLOW_DRAWPIXELS 1`. This will dramatically speed up responsiveness on partial alpha background planes.

SNAPPING TO THE ELUSIVE CAMERA PIVOT

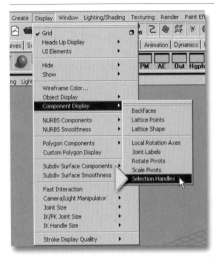

Often you may find yourself wanting to add something to an already animated camera, such as a flock of birds, a camera holdout matte, or a flying hot dog for a commercial. Grouping under a camera is easy, but often there are no points in which to snap to. To make the camera pivot visible and ready for snapping, start by selecting the camera and choose Display, Component Display, Selection Handles. Now a handle will appear that can be snapped to using the point snap mode.

STREAMLINING DEPTH OF FIELD

Camera depth of field is both a timeless emulation of optics as well as a trendy and transitory effect of the moment, similar to the lens flare boom years ago. There are many ways to achieve DOF, some more accurate but expensive and some cheaper to render and less accurate. Maya integrates DOF in the Camera Attribute Editor under the Depth of Field menu. It is useful in that it provides a basic rendition of DOF for a bit of expense, but it is fairly tough to adjust the center of focus properly by guesswork. To make this step easier, we can use the Connection Editor to link two attributes in the camera. Start by MMB-clicking on the camera icon in the Multilister or Hypershade. This calls up the Connection Editor, where we need to choose Center of Interest in the left column and Focus Distance in the right. Now if you select the camera and turn on the Manip Mode using the hotkey "T," you can adjust the Center of Interest manipulator to the area desired to be held in focus, and all is good in the world once again.

MOTION BLUR CHOICES

Motion blur is one of those seemingly minor aspects of rendering that is in fact one of the most important aspects of a renderer. In the film world, renderers live and die by motion blur performance and quality. In Maya, there are two choices—3D and 2D motion blur. 3D is much more expensive and artifact-prone render-wise but offers more realistic blur and control per object. 2D is a post-process that consumes significant RAM, but it is generally faster and preferable for most jobs. Another nice feature of 2D is the Keep Motion Vectors option in the Render Global Settings, Motion Blur menu. This enables a 2D post-process using the command line blur2d executable after rendering is complete in order to tweak the result. Type `blur2d -h` to see options in a DOS shell. Another nifty trick to use with standalone 2D motion blur is that you can use it to blur footage that was not rendered in Maya. Also, an invisible object in Maya still saves vectors, so if you have an image sequence mapped to the image plane, a totally transparent object with 2D motion blur can be used to smudge the image plane. You might also use this to smudge shadows that do not utilize motion blur or for some other kind of creative effect. The last option is to use a third-party motion blur application that inspects frames for 2D pixel travel and provides a reasonable alternative as well.

3D STEREOSCOPIC RENDERING

3D stereoscopic rendering seems to be the rage again for novel film experiences. Not since the 50s have we seen so many audiences wearing 3D glasses, except this time around they are wearing techy infrared full-color polarized glasses with surround sound on Imax screens. Who knew we'd have it so good? Of course, much of this revival is due to 3D rendering's ease of creating stereo imagery. Doing stereo animation properly requires a sophisticated camera setup in Maya and a decent method of playback and viewing, but here is an easy way to get your feet wet: First animate a camera over 8 frames with what would be a few inches to a few feet of spread from screen left to right. Render these 8 frames and use a handy Photoshop action called Anaglyph_Action.atn (found free online) to try frames 1 to 4 as left eye and 5 to 8 as the right eye to find the proper "interoccular distance," or eye spread. With that action, the red/blue compositing is done effortlessly and will deliver a beautiful result with red/blue glasses. For the next step, try a StereoJet polarized print for full-color rendition. Or go all the way and try a 3D remake of *House of Wax* on stereo Imax.

LEVEL OF DETAIL TRICKERY

The game industry has learned the value of using level of detail (LOD) models for many years. LODs allow you to have highly detailed models when near the camera and lesser detailed models when distant from the camera, as well as multiple levels of details in between the two extremes. By working this way, you can expect to navigate around in your scene much faster due to fewer polygons in the viewport that otherwise would need to be rendered. Maya can easily let you build this feature into your scene. First, the LOD models should be present in the scene, naming the group prefixes something like LOD-hi, LOD-mid, and LOD-low. Next select the highest detailed LOD model first and select Edit, Level of Detail, Group. Now open the Outliner and note a new icon has been added with the name lodgroup1, but feel free to rename the node. Now, with the middle mouse button, drag the next LOD into that group, and then the next LOD, until they are all added. Select the top-most group node. You will see some new controls in the Channel Box editor. Next, put distances into the threshold boxes for each object to transition to the next LOD. Now with everything set up, when the camera dollies in and out, you should see your objects swap between each of the LODs in real time.

BUILDING A 3D CAMERA ENVELOPE

This tip is designed to help keep large scenes with animated cameras as efficient as possible, by retaining only the geometry that is seen in the camera's view, and allowing deletion of what is never seen by the camera. A good example of this is building a city layout where you want to place a car on an animated path through the city streets with a camera to represent the point of view (POV) of the driver. Why take the overhead of all those buildings you'll never see, and how will you know which buildings are never in the camera throughout the animation without having to check every frame? Here's how. First, set up your entire scene with an animated camera. Now, select your camera from your panel menu View, Select Camera. Next, display your camera's film gate with View, Camera Settings, Film Gate. Then, create a box and scale it out from the camera lens to the farthest object in the scene. Looking through the camera, scale the box out to align with the camera's film gate. Looking from a perspective view you should now have a large trapezoid attached to the front of your camera representing your field of view, and at this point, you should parent the box to your camera.

To create the actual 3D envelope of your camera, you have to create an animated snapshot of the camera along the path with Animate, Create Animation Snapshot, Options. You should now have a series of trapezoids that move along the spline representing your camera's field of view. You can safely delete any object outside and not intersecting the trapezoidal path.

GOING THE DISTANCE

Whether working with lights or cameras, it's always a good idea to know how far away they are from their target objects or main points of interest in the scene. This information will be very handy when you have to deal with depth of field, clipping plane distances, light falloff, and so forth. A great way to approach this is by constraining a Distance Tool to your lights or cameras in the scene. Here's how to set this up. First, you set up your light or camera into your scene. Then, you bring in your measurement tool from the Create, Measure Tools, Distance Tool. Snap the first point to the light or camera, and then the second point to where you would like the target point to rest. The next step is to parent the camera or light to the distance tool locator. Now when you move your lights or camera around in your scene, they will always reflect a precise distance from their target points.

YOU'RE CROSSING THE LINE THERE, BUDDY

Learning the language and conventions of film is critical to doing camerawork that feels correct and mature. Trying to cover editing in a paragraph is unreasonable, but one principle that many beginning animators often overlook is that of "crossing the line." Covering conversation or interaction between two individuals should generally be held to one side of the "conversation line," the axis formed between the two. So, one shot could be looking over the shoulder of one to the other and vice versa, but just not on opposite sides of the line. This minimizes disorientation for the viewer, but on occasion, the line needs to be crossed for some spatial reason. In this case, one can track the camera across the line actively or insert a cutaway shot to secondary objects or characters before crossing.

Building
Character
(Animation That Is)

Character animation has led the charge in CGI evolution for several years now. It has driven ahead the explosive success of CGI in feature film effects, and the ambition to create persuasive and compelling human performance

Building Character (Animation, That Is)

more than skin-deep

Contributions by Erick Miller and Kenneth Ibrahim

remains the Holy Grail that drives animators and directors forward. Conversely, the success of a 3D package in the market has largely hinged on how well it has supported this aim by providing tools of sufficient depth and flexibility for character work. Hands down, Maya overtook the industry rapidly by providing a very flexible and rich toolset squarely aimed at the goal of supporting the complexities and vagaries of character animation. New features in version 6.0 such as Motion Retargeting, updated Trax, or Hair creation make previously tedious tasks simple affairs. However, character animation is one of the more technical and involved subjects to learn in Maya, and therefore it does require a deep capacity to embrace technical issues and minutia. As an entrance test, you might ask yourself if 12:00 is flashing on your home VCR—if not, that is a good sign that you should venture forward. Doing character animation well is also a lifelong study because the technical issues are only the means to an end. The following tips should assist you in this journey into the deeper waters of Maya.

GETTING ORIENTED WITH YOUR JOINTS

Creating joints is the way you build a skeleton for a character so that your character can transform from a rigid model into an animated character. To make joints, go to Skeleton, Joint Tool. You can start creating a portion of your character's skeleton by clicking in the view port with the Joint Tool and using the middle mouse button to lay the joints in the exact spot you want them. You can then create new portions of the skeleton and parent them to the appropriate joint by selecting the child and then the parent and hitting the "p" key. After you have laid out your character's skeleton, it is vital that the orientation of each joint is appropriate for the type of joint that it may be on the character's body. For example, the hip joint, which rotates the entire leg upward and around, should have its rotation axis oriented in such a way that one axis points forward in front of the character, and the other points to the side. You can edit the local rotation axis of the joint by selecting the joint, going into component mode (hit the F8 key), right-click selecting the pick mask that looks like a question mark, and choosing Local Rotation Axes. You can then edit these components by selecting and rotating them. After you have them oriented perfectly to your liking, be sure to select all your joints and execute the MEL command in the command line:

```
joint -e -zso -ch;
```

This will align all your scale orientations with your rotate orients, which is quite important if you ever want to scale your joints. Finally, you want to try to avoid gimbal lock as much as possible. Gimbal lock is the phenomenon common to Euler rotations, when two rotation axes get lined up perfectly with each other and cause you to lose an axis of rotation. A good start to fighting gimbal lock is to set your rotation to gimbal mode by double-clicking on the Rotate Tool from the Toolbox and choosing gimbal. Next, open up the Attribute Editor for each joint and experiment with different rotate orders by clicking under the Transform Attributes section of the joint and choosing different rotate orders from the drop-down selection menus. To get the best rotation order least likely to cause the character to get into gimbal lock, simply rotate the joint and see if a 90-degree rotation causes the other two axes to get lined up with each other. If it does, then try a new rotation order.

FK, IK, OK?

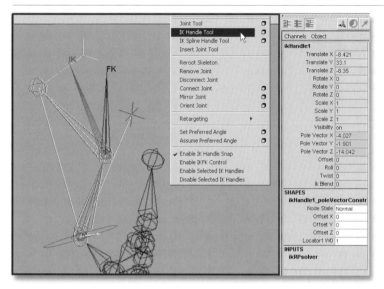

IK, otherwise known as Inverse Kinematics, is really not as complicated as it sounds. In fact, it doesn't really get any simpler! IK handles just enable you to attach a control to, say, an arm or a leg, which then creates a handle that you can grab and animate with. After you create an IK handle, you can translate the hand or foot around, and the angles of all the parent joints rotate into proper resulting positions—that's the mathematical calculation being performed by the IK solver. IK is great when you want to lock a hand or foot down onto a location and have the rest of the skeleton animate around it, like, for example, if a character was on the ground doing push-ups. To create an IK handle, go to the Skeleton menu and select IK Handle Tool. Next, simply select the parent joint (shoulder) and then the child joint (wrist) of your character, and an IK handle will be created automatically. The built-in capability to blend from IK to FK is a part of the new solver and is an addition that seems quite promising. To blend from IK to FK, simply change the attribute IkBlend from zero to one. You can then animate in the FK mode of the skeleton by simply selecting it and setting keys. One other thing that is really important when dealing with IK setups is stable control over the center joint (elbow). You can always animate the twist attribute on the IK handle, but oftentimes it is better to have a control there that you can select and animate. You can create a control for the center joint by creating a locator and positioning it somewhere on the side that the center joint bends toward, and then selecting the locator first, then the IK handle, and choosing Constrain, Pole Vector.

SMOOTH SKINNING HOTKEYS FOR PAINTING WEIGHTS

After you have set up and rigged your character, it is time to make it deform. Smooth skinning is the better, more sophisticated binding tool of choice (Skin, Bind Skin, Smooth Bind), but painting the weights of your smooth bound character can be more like wading through an endless sea of joint names. But, it doesn't have to be that way! There are a few quick tips and Artisan hotkeys that will, without a doubt, speed up your weight painting efforts. First, always remember that you can paint or assign weights on a per-vertex level simply by selecting the vertices of the geometry and then entering the paint weights tool (Skin, Edit Smooth Skin, Paint Skin Weights Tool). When you're within the tool, you can use the Flood option to fill all the vertices you have

selected with a single value. You can therefore weight single vertices this way, without the painful old-fashioned way of having to open up the Component Editor, sort through the long, ugly list of vertices, and then type numbers by hand. Second, there is a great set of already defined Artisan hotkeys for painting that saves huge amounts of time, streamlining the weight painting process. Here are some really helpful ones:

- Right-click over a joint and choose Paint Weights to paint weights for that joint. No more scrolling through an endless list of confusing joint names!
- Hold down the "U" key and left-click to choose your painting mode.
- Hold down the "N" key and left-click and drag to activate a virtual slider to change your painting value (between zero and one).
- Hold down the "B" key and left-click and drag to change the brush size.

After you get used to painting weights on a per-vertex level and using these little-known default Maya hotkeys, your ease and speed of painting weights should be quickly increased.

PLEASE CONSTRAIN YOURSELF

Constraints could easily be one of the most commonly used rigging tools, second only to Joints and IK. One of the slickest ways to control an object with constraints is to take advantage of the fact that constraints are weighted, meaning that each constraint of the same type (point, orient, and so on) on an object gets averaged with the other constraints of that type, based on each one of the constraint weights. If a constraint weight is zero, then that constraint has zero influence or control. If a constraint weight is one, then it gets equally averaged with all the other constraints. You can easily achieve a blending effect from one object to another by having two constraints and simply animating one of the weight attributes from one to zero and the other weight attribute from zero to one at the same time. There are many uses for such a technique, such as blending between multiple skeletal setups, like from an IK setup, into a special dynamics setup, and then perhaps into a motion capture setup. Another great use for blending constraint weights is to pick up objects and attach them to a character's hand or body. Constraints always operate as though they are in world space; that means that if you ever have a node that is being controlled by a parent transform, the constraint will take precedence over the parent. Point and orient constraints also have a relatively new attribute called Offset. By using the constraint's offset attribute, you can layer additional motion on top of the constraint in an additive manner, which lets you offset the constraint to any position you need. So, multiple constraint weights are the way to go. Whenever you need to blend from one transform space to another, don't dismay, constrain!

NOT YOUR GRANDFATHER'S UTILITY NODES

While setting up a character, chances are that at some point you will find yourself needing or wanting to add some simple math into your character rig. Your first instinct may be to open up the Expression Editor and pound out a quick little expression that perhaps multiplies or adds two values and then maybe divides them by another. Traditionally, using expressions would be the way to go, but there are a few disadvantages with expressions that can become obvious over time. For one, the hard-coded node names that get embedded inside of expressions can potentially cause them to break when the nodes get renamed. Second, they can be a bit slow, depending on what they are calculating, because they need to be evaluated on the fly. So, what is a good solution? Use utility nodes! Those very same nodes that for some odd reason are labeled only for rendering can prove to be a character setup artist's best friend. Go to Window, Rendering Editors, Multilister. When the Multilister is open, go to Edit, Create. When the Create Render Node window is open, click on the tab furthest to the right, titled Utilities. Beneath this tab is a plethora of hidden treasures for character setup. Just to get started, there's the plusMinusAverage node, the multiplyDivide node, and the vectorProduct node, all of which immediately give you the capability to calculate all sorts of vector math, such as dot products and cross products. The condition node, the reverse node, and the clamp node can also prove quite handy in times when one would otherwise resort to bulky expressions. The time has now come for the world to recognize the immense power of utility nodes as character setup tools!

SQUASH AND STRETCH EXPRESSIONS

In this example, we will create a simple expression that uses a function for maintaining elliptical volume. One of the first rules for writing fast and efficient mathematical expressions for character setup is that you never want to directly evaluate MEL procedures that will hook data into your rig through an expression. You *can* do this, but it is much better to do straight variable assignment to attribute values. Doing this causes the expression node to actually create incoming attribute connections to the nodes that you are using to retrieve values in the expression. For example, doing something like this in an expression:

```
$value = nurbsSphere1.scaleX;
```

causes the expression node itself to connect the scaleX attribute of the sphere directly to one of its internal input attributes (.input[0] in this case). This is desired behavior because the expression node itself can keep track of the data as direct attribute connections between dependency data and doesn't need to perform as much evaluation in order to output the math within the expression. Try not to call a getAttr from within an expression (unless you are prepared for some potential problems, such as name changes that break the expression and create sluggishness). Of course there are some perfectly valid times to use heavy MEL within an expression, but for attribute assignment to variables, never use getAttr if you don't need to. Here is a simple example of integrating a simple formula into a mathematical expression. Notice the differences between expressions and MEL, such as variable type definition and direct attribute assignment being tied to variable definitions. Also note the direct use of the variable name in the square root function; it is not necessary to call getAttr because the expression will automatically calculate the attribute value internally much faster by using the attribute name directly. So, try this out:

```
sphere;
$PI = 3.14159265358979323846264;
$squash = sqrt ( ($PI*3*4) * (4*$PI/3) ) / ( 4*$PI* nurbsSphere1.scaleY );
nurbsSphere1.scaleX = $squash;
nurbsSphere1.scaleZ = $squash;
```

Next, try to scale the sphere along the Y axis using the .scaleY, which is the attribute that drives the expression. Expressions can be extremely powerful for character rigging when used properly.

SCRIPTING YOUR SETUP

```
M Script Editor                                          _□×
File  Edit  Script  Help
select -r baseSpineJoint.rotatePivot endSpineJoint.rotatePivot ;
string $result[] = `ikHandle -sol ikSplineSolver`;
string $cvs[] = `ls -fl ($result[2]+".cv[*]")` ;
for($cv in $cvs)
{
        cluster $cv;
};
// Warning: Some items cannot be moved in the 3D view. //
select -cl  ;

select -r baseSpineJoint.rotatePivot endSpineJoint.rotatePivot ;
string $result[] = `ikHandle -sol ikSplineSolver`;
string $cvs[] = `ls -fl ($result[2]+".cv[*]")` ;
for($cv in $cvs)
{
        cluster $cv;
}
◄□                                                        ►
```

MEL Scripting is useful in so many ways. One of the really great ways to use MEL is to create MEL scripts that automate the character setup process. What this means is to create macro style scripts that call built-in MEL functions as well as other MEL scripts that have been written with the sole purpose of performing the character setup process. The benefits of creating an automatically scripted setup are two-fold. First, the process of rigging can sometimes be complex and confusing and is often quite involved, but if you script the setup, you can always have that script available to go back to or to reuse in other cases. Second, scripting the character setup should be done in such a way that if the geometry or even the joints that are being set up change later, the automatic scripted setup will still work. This means that even if the character changed drastically after you set it up, the setup itself would not need to change. This is a huge time-saver, especially if the character runs the risk of needing a redesign that would otherwise force a redesign of the rig as well.

A very simple example of creating a scripted setup would be taking a set of joints, adding a spine IK to them, and then creating a cluster for each CV on the spline IK curve:

```
select -r baseSpineJoint.rotatePivot endSpineJoint.rotatePivot ;
string $result[] = `ikHandle -sol ikSplineSolver`;
string $cvs[] = `ls -fl ($result[2]+".cv[*]")` ;
for($cv in $cvs)
{
cluster $cv;
```

BULGING BICEPS WITH SCULPT DEFORMERS

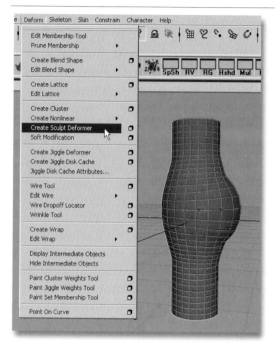

Sculpt deformers are one of the coolest nonlinear deformers in Maya because of their stable, yet extremely fast and dynamic-looking layered deformation capabilities. Sculpt deformers are best to use on layered skinned characters or layered on top of geometry that is first deformed into place using some sort of linear deformer. The reason is that sculpt deformers can create interesting ellipsoidal bulging deformations across the surface geometry, but they will never give you the straightforward deformation that a joint bound to a skin cluster will when you are posing to a mesh. Instead, you can parent the sculpt deformer objects under the transforms of joints, scale the sculpt objects down to the proper size, and create all sorts of bulging effects using set driven keys or expressions that create the appearance of an object that is sliding beneath the geometry.

Create a polygon cylinder with enough resolution in the cylinder for it to deform nicely. Select the cylinder and then go to the Deform menu, Create Sculpt Deformer. Now, you should have a big bulge in your cylinder. Take a look in your 3D view and look at the nodes in the Hypergraph. You will see that there is a sphere-shaped sculpt object, and there is also a locator right at the center of the sphere. Select them both and scale them until there is a nice-looking bulge in your object. Now, play with some of the attributes in the Channel Box on the sculpt node. Maximum Displacement will cause a bulge that extends out more, and Dropoff Distance will cause a larger gradient between the origin of the sculpt object and its elliptically extended borders. The locator that is created is best kept as a child of the sculpt sphere, exactly at the center of the sculpt object, although slightly offsetting it can cause some nice angular sliding. Thus, this is just a general rule and is meant to be broken to create certain effects. Also note that NURBS geometry can be used as a sculpt deformer, which adds further possibilities.

BLENDSHAPE FACIALS

Setting up blendshapes for facial animation is a process that can take thoughtful planning as far as what the shapes should be to get controllable facial targets. When setting out to model facial targets to create blend shapes, think about how the shapes will layer with each other. At the heart of a blendshape is a really simple, entirely linear and additive equation. It takes each vertex point position being blended in and first subtracts it from the original position to calculate an offset. Next, it just multiplies that offset by the weight value that is meant to be animated and then literally adds all the values together with all the other weighted offsets from the other shape models that are currently connected to the blendshape. Although this yields a straight line from vertex position to vertex position, it also yields an extremely predictable and appealing result. With this in mind, think about the shapes and how they layer together when setting out to model blendshapes. Here is a good list to start from when modeling face shapes. Each one of these models can and should most likely be split up into left, right, upper, and lower, depending on the shape itself and the portion of the face it affects:

- **Phonemes:** Aah, Eee/Iii, Ohh/Oow, Fff, Sss, Ddd, Gga, Cha/Shh
- **Emotions:** Happy/smile, sad/upset, angry, annoyed, disgusted, surprised, confused
- **Additive separate shapes:** Brow up/down/furrow, blink, eyes wide/squint, snarl, nose flare, cheek up/down/toward center/away from center, lip pucker/flattened/squashed together, each lip up/down/toward center/away from center, each lip curl in/out, each corner up/down/toward center/away from center, entire mouth slanted side to side

As you are modeling each shape, it is important to test how they work with each other, which is a vital part of modeling face shapes. Finally, remember that when you add blendshapes into a model that is already deforming (say with a jaw joint for example), be sure to use the Deformation Order option from the Blendshape Options window in the Advanced tab and set it to Front of Chain.

WRAP DEFORMERS

The purpose of a wrap deformer is to use a lower-resolution mesh to drive the deformations of a higher-resolution mesh. This way, you can do many things much faster, such as skinning, weighting, and making updates to the final high-resolution geometry, all without affecting the actual weights that have been painted or the vertex ordering of the final deforming mesh. Wrap deformers' only drawback is that they can be somewhat slow to calculate, especially on the initial binding calculation for a high-res mesh. First, create a polygon cylinder, with settings of Subdivisions Axis at 20 and Subdivisions Height at 10. Next, create a lower-resolution cylinder, this time setting the Subdivisions Axis to 8 and Subdivisions Height to 3. Now, delete history and freeze transformations on all. Next, use Skeleton, Joint Tool, and put the lower joint at the bottom of the cylinders, the center joint at the center of the cylinders, and the top joint at the top of the cylinders. Finally, bind the low-resolution cylinder to the joints using smooth skinning (Skin, Bind Skin, Smooth Bind), being extra careful not to select the higher-resolution mesh when you perform the bind. Select nothing, then select the high-resolution mesh first and the low-resolution mesh second, and then perform Deform, Create Wrap. You should now have a wrap deformer that you can play with that should deform the higher resolution mesh by rotating the joints on the lower resolution mesh. Finally, you can tweak some of the attributes to get a performance gain on the wrap deformer. For example, you can set the Weight Threshold attribute value all the way to one. This will sacrifice the nice, smoothed, rounded deformations on the high-resolution model, and in places low-resolution edges will bend, but it will increase performance of the wrap deformer itself by quite a bit. You also can tweak Max Distance, which is the maximum distance that the deformer should use to determine how far away the low-resolution object will ever be from the high-resolution object at the time the wrap deformer node is created. Tweaking this attribute to its bare minimum can also improve performance on the wrap deformer.

FLOWING DOWN THE PATH

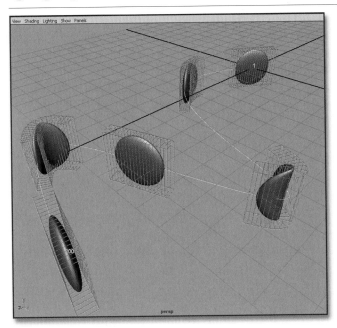

A common animation technique is to set an object to a motion path to choreograph its translation. A not-so-common variation of this technique is to use Flow Paths, a nifty trick where a lattice is translated along with the object, but whose local axes of each set of points follows the curve, thus deforming along the way and influencing the host object as well. This is clearly useful for fish swimming but can be applied to any squash animation technique. Start by creating a NURBS sphere and scaling z at .2. Draw a CV curve that contains some sharp corners originating at the sphere location. Rotate the sphere in y with the slender side aligned with the curve. Next, select the sphere and then Shift-click to select the curve. Choose Animate, Motion Paths, Attach to Motion Path options. Make sure Follow is checked, orient the Front Axis to x, and then choose Attach. Play it back to check proper path animation. Now select the sphere, then curve again, and choose Animate, Motion Paths, Flow Path Object options. Choose 10 Front Divisions and press Flow. Now the sphere will follow the contours of the curve. Note that the options enable the lattice to be attached to the object or the entire curve for very precise deformations.

CYCLE THOSE CURVES

In the Graph Editor, curves are manipulated to establish the animation of an object. One way to reduce the setting of redundant keys involves using the cycle options in the Graph Editor. Create a few basic keys on a curve and then choose Graph Editor, Curves, Post Infinity, Cycle. The curve will repeat indefinitely, but to view it, choose Graph Editor, View, Infinity. Now try the other options such as Linear, where the final tangent is shot into infinity, enabling two keys anywhere in time to establish speed. The option of Cycle with Offset will cycle but stack the next on top of the last, creating an escalating effect.

FREE THEN BREAK YOUR TANGENTS

Getting good results by simply manipulating keys in the Graph Editor can often be good enough, but to really provide subtle control over your motion, use the full array of tangent tools available. Start by creating a few keys, then select the curve and choose Graph Editor, Curves, Weighted Tangents.

This will enable more precise control over what are normally simple tangent handles. Next, select a key and then select Keys, Free Tangent Weight as well as Keys, Break Tangents. Now each tangent handle is controlled much as a Bézier curve is in illustration packages. Not only is this method more intuitive, but it also can be used to create very subtle or dramatic curves that the default methods cannot.

FLAP YOUR WINGS WITH EXPRESSION

If you are new to expressions, here is a good introduction to them and a reason that you might use one—that of a bird flapping its wings. For our example, we will use simple spheres, but feel free to consult your local Audubon Society chapter for modeling help. Start by constructing three spheres, one rounded for the body and two flattened for wings. Locate the pivot points of the wings just inside the body. Name the wings right_wing and left_wing and parent under the body node named Boid. Now open the Expression Editor under Window, Animation Editors. Call the Expression Name wing_flapping and insert this in the main expression field:

```
right_wing.rotateZ=sin(time*10)*10;
left_wing.rotateZ=sin(time*10)*10;
```

The first value of 10 is the rate of flapping (per second) and the other 10 is the amount of rotation in degrees. Change these to suit your preferences. To add an attribute that provides easier control and possible keyframing of this rate, pick the body node and under the Attribute Editor, choose Attributes, Add Attributes. Call the Attribute Name flap_speed and set Minimum to 0, Maximum to 40, and Default to 10. Now update the expression to this:

```
right_wing.rotateZ=sin(time*Boid.flap_speed)*10;
left_wing.rotateZ=sin(time*Boid.4flap_speed)*10;
```

Use the new slider in Boid's Attribute Editor, Extra Attributes to key or make other connections to other expressions.

GRAPH EDITOR EXPRESSIONS

The Graph Editor offers access to keyframes primarily, but it does offer simple viewing of expressions, which can give useful information if needed. Select the Boid node created in the previous tip and open the Graph Editor. Choose View, Show Results. Open the hierarchy in the Graph Editor Outliner and select the RotateZ of either the left or right wing. A sine wave should appear, but note that it is not editable without using Curves, Bake Channel. Note also that some complex expressions may tax the Graph Editor, so the Show Results options offer different sampling rates for dealing with this issue.

FINDING THOSE RECLUSIVE LOCAL AXES

Here is a function that is hidden away in a nook that many may overlook. Frequently, a local axis may need to be oriented differently from default for animation purposes. There is no command for this, so here is how to do it: Select the object in question and then go to the Component mode selection menu. Right-click on the question mark to display the object's local axis. When selected, it is available for rotation through the standard Rotate command. Note that translation of the local axis is not available here because the local pivot would need to be altered (that is, the use of the Insert key) to allow for that.

PROMPTING MULTIPLE KEYFRAMES

Here's a great little timesaver when you need to set many keys across a span of time. Go to Animate, Set Key Options and check Set Keys At Prompt. Press Set Key, and a small menu will appear that will enable you to input a range of individual frames to which you may set keys. To determine to which attribute you are setting keys, use Set Keys on Current Manipulator Handle while the axis you are interested in is clicked on to be active.

   BREAKDOWN YOUR KEYS

One handy feature in the Graph Editor you may have missed is the use of Breakdown keys. A variation of standard keys, Breakdown keys are keys put in a different state where they are influenced by the position and value of neighboring keys, making modification of sets of keys much easier. Begin with a curve containing multiple keys.

Select a few internal keys that have neighbors and then choose Keys, Convert to Breakdown or right-click over one to find the same command. Now select a neighboring key and move it in time and notice how the Breakdown keys respond by scaling appropriately. When done, convert back to standard keys with Keys, Convert to Keys.

DRIVING MISS DRIVEN KEY

Maya has a few tricks up its sleeve that other packages may not. One example of this is Set Driven Key, which essentially is expressions for lazy people. Not that that is a bad thing, of course. Set Driven Key simply connects one animated attribute to another so that one acts upon the other. It goes one step further in that it maps out that relationship to an editable curve so that the relationship between the two can be refined and optimized. Start by creating a sphere and a cube scaled into a long box. Raise the sphere above the cube and select the sphere. Choose Animate, Set Driven Key, Set options. While the sphere is selected, choose Load Driver, select the box, and select Load Driven. Highlight translateY of the sphere and rotateY of the box. Press Key, raise the sphere in Y, rotate the box a few revolutions in Y, and then press Key again. Now as you raise the sphere, it will spin the box rapidly. To edit the resultant curve, pick the box and open the Graph Editor. Now timings and eases can be set easily. Remember, the power in Set Driven Key is to link any number of attributes together in complex ways with relative ease.

TEXTURE MAP YOUR ANIMATION

Here is a genuine Killer Tip for creating random functions from 2D textures for animation channels of objects. Start by creating a sphere and opening the Attribute Editor, as this hook will not be accessible through the Channel Box attribute fields. Right-click in the Translate Y channel field and choose Create New Texture. Pick a 2D Fractal Texture and turn on the Animated check box in Fractal Attributes. Playback of the timeline will not yet create motion, though, because we need to provide keyframing of the Time field or simply place a simple expression such as =time/25 directly into the field. After that is entered, play back for erratic motion. Now modulate fractal parameters such as Ratio for smoothness or Alpha Gain or Offset for intensity. Other options exist similarly with the 2D Noise Texture, which has interesting options such as Perlin, Billow, Wave, or the intriguingly named Space-Time.

   TIME SLIDER TRICKS

Setting keys in Maya is typically done by right-clicking to Set Key in an attribute field or perhaps by using the keyframe hotkeys such as "S" (key all keyable fields), Shift-W (key translations), Shift-E (key rotations), or Shift-R (key scaling). Many artists, however, fail to consider that the timeline itself offers various conveniences for keyframing. Start by Shift-clicking on a red key indicator in the timeline. Two arrows appear, enabling movement of the keys within the timeline and saving a trip to the Graph Editor. Now Shift-click on a collection of keys and note that new arrows are added in the outer edges to scale the collection in or out, while the inner arrows can translate all together. Lastly, move the slider to a red marker or keyframe that you want to delete and right-click to find a pop-up menu that has a variety of useful hidden functions, including delete. This will save gas and reduce time-consuming trips to your local Graph Editor.

RECORDING YOUR MOUSE

Here is a hidden gem tucked well away in Maya. Often it could be helpful to use mouse movement to create animation curves in order to provide a "handheld" feel or establish erratic motion to objects or attributes. Deep inside MEL is a node called the Record Node that will facilitate such a trick. It is basically a node that will record mouse actions as keyframed curves and pipe those curves into an attribute of another node. After data is captured, the Record Node can be deleted. Start by entering this bit of MEL to set it up:

```
sphere;
createNode record;
connectAttr nurbsSphere1.ty record1.input;
```

Now set your playback speed in the Animation Preferences to 15 fps in order to avoid out-distancing the record process. Begin the capture with this command:

```
play -record;
```

Now move the mouse erratically in order to move the sphere in y translation. After a few seconds, use the Esc key to stop the recording and view the resultant curve in the Graph Editor. Other attributes can have concurrent connections as well to save cutting and pasting of curves. Bear in mind that the attributes chosen can be much broader than just translations.

PREFIX YOUR JOINTS

This is one of those tips that can really make a difference, especially when creating a complex bone/joint system for an intricate character model. The Prefix tool can be found under Modify, Prefix Hierarchy Names, which will add a prefix name of your choice to the selected object and carry it down the hierarchical chain to all the children nodes. A good example of this would be if you have already created a joint/bone system and you wanted to change the default naming convention from `joint1, joint2, joint3`, and so on to something like this: `Left-leg_joint1, Left-leg_joint2, Right-leg_joint1, Right-leg_joint2`, and so on. When it's time to animate, you'll be glad you did this.

MAKE IT LIVE

This hidden gem is great for those times when one needs to build onto an already existing model where the new geometry needs to contour to the old. With Make Live, reverse engineering a model is so much easier, by making the geometry a template that acts as a 3D drawing plane. Now when curves are drawn, they are actually clinging to the Make Live surface as if it were a magnet. Even after laying down the curves, the points can be adjusted while still contouring to the surface. Make Live is accessible through the menu tabs, under Modify, Make Live. To make an existing live object not live, just navigate back to the Modify menu tab, and it should now read as Make Not Live. Note that one will get better results with this on NURBS versus polys.

PLAYBLAST SELECTED FRAMES

Playblast has always been a valuable tool in Maya, especially for animators. Having the ability to play back an animation or a large scene that might not be able to play in real time through the viewport otherwise is crucial. Playblast screen-captures the selected viewport and writes out a series of images or animation, which then gets called back up in either FCheck or a media player for playback in real time. That's all fine, but what if only certain frames are desired, and not the whole animation? With version 6.0, a simple MEL command can solve this problem. For example:

```
playblast -frame 5 -frame 32 -frame 51
```

This will output only frames 5, 32, and 51 of your current animation to Playblast.

REDIRECTING MOTION

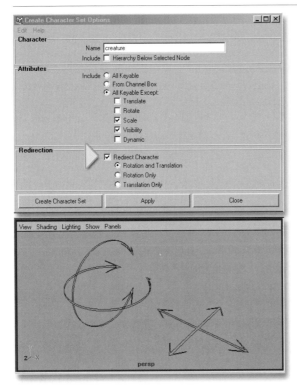

Now, easier than ever, you can redirect motion within an animation anywhere and anytime. Redirecting motion allows you to modify a character's path or orientation at any point during its animation. For example, you may have a character that has been animated along a path, but now you would like to see this character facing the opposite direction and off to one side when it reaches the end of the path. To make a character redirectable, select the root of the character set whose motion you want redirected, and then navigate to Character, Create Character Set, Options. In the Create Character Set, Options menu, set the attributes as desired, but be sure to turn on Redirect Character. You can choose to redirect the rotation only, the translation only, or both. After selecting "Apply the rotation and/or translation", redirection controls appear at the root of the current character. Place them where you would like the pivot point to be, and then set a keyframe. The next step is to make the object redirectable by selecting Character, Redirect. This will place new rotation and/or translation redirection controls at the pivot of the object. Continue to reposition and set keyframes for both the rotation and translation controls at the points of motion you would like redirected.

PAINT FX BRUSH FOR HAIR

If you're looking for a quick and easy way to add hair to your models, try the new Paint FX brush for hair. Make your surface paintable, and start painting the surface with the hair you have always wanted. It's that easy. You can even control every aspect of the hair's attribute through the channel box editor. You control how shiny, curly, or bouncy it is, and can even animate its growth over a period of time. The Paint FX brush for hair can be found under Window, Paint Effects. When the Paint Effects window opens, click on the Brush tab and choose Get Brush. This will open the Visor window panel, and from there you can select the hair folder, giving you a variety of hairstyles to choose from.

USING POINTPOSITION TO TRACK OBJECTS TO COMPONENTS

Point constraining one object to another in Maya is a snap, but if you want to point constrain an object to the component of another object (for example, CVs or vertices), we turn to MEL. The `pointPosition` command returns the translation values of any type of point, including vertices, CVs, and particles, in either local or worldspace. This can be used in an expression to update the position of an object based on the translation of another's component. To see the command in action, create a polygon sphere, select one of its vertices, and run the pointPosition command from the Script Editor window as follows:

```
pointPosition;
```

You should see the world space position values returned for the selected CV. This mechanism can be used to arrange geometry into interesting patterns or for very simple particle instancing, to name a couple of applications. Here's an example: Create a polygonal sphere named "baseFrame" with a radius of 10 and set both the Subdivisions Axis and Subdivisions Height attributes to 4. This gives us a mesh consisting of 14 vertices. Next, create 14 default NURBS spheres named "ns0" through "ns13" and map them to each of the "baseFrame" object's vertices by entering the following expression in the Expression Editor:

```
// retrieve the number of vertices in the frame object
int $i, $numVerts[] = `polyEvaluate -v baseFrame`;
float $pos[3];

// retrieve the position of each vertex and
// move the corresponding sphere there
for($i=0; $i<$numVerts[0]; $i++)
{
        $pos = pointPosition("baseFrame.vtx[" + $i + "]");
        move -a $pos[0] $pos[1] $pos[2] ("ns" + $i);
}
```

The expression loops over each vertex in the mesh and uses the move command to place the corresponding sphere at the coordinates returned by the pointPosition command. Because this is an expression, the "baseFrame" object can be animated and the NURBS spheres will follow. Note that they will only follow the cube when the timeline is playing and not when you are interactively moving the cube.

CONSTRAIN ONE OBJECT TO ANOTHER USING THE XFORM COMMAND

```
Script Editor                                              _ □ ×
File   Edit   Script   Help
xform -q -worldSpace -matrix nc1;
// Result: 0.53468 -1.168758 0.0709492 0 2.049844 0.770313 -2.758336 0 0.899852
xform -m 0.53468 -1.168758 0.0709492 0 2.049844 0.770313 -2.758336 0 0.899852 0

xform -q -worldSpace -matrix nc1;

xform -m 0.53468 -1.168758 0.0709492 0 2.049844 0.770313 -2.758336 0 0.899852 0
```

Whereas the previous tip demonstrated how to constrain an object to a component using the pointPosition command, this tip explains how the xform command can be used to match the transformations of one object to that of another. In essence you can perform a point, orient, and scale constraint all at once! Here's how. Create a NURBS cone called nc1 and transform it any way you like. You can even parent it to other objects with transforms of their own. Then, create another NURBS cone called nc2 and type the following command:

```
xform -q -worldSpace -matrix nc1;
```

This returns the composite transformation matrix of the object in world space as 16 individual float values (the row and column values of the matrix). In other words, it defines the translation, rotation, and scale of the object. You can take these values and apply them to the second object, again using xform as follows:

```
xform -m 0.53468 -1.168758 0.0709492 0 2.049844 0.770313 -2.758336 0 0.899852
0.460056 0.797199 0 -13.217321 6.6293 -16.896341 1 nc2;
```

These happen to be the values from my scene file and yours of course will be different. To make this more programmatic, you can store the return values from the first xform call and then use them in the second call by their increasing array index number. This would look like:

```
float $mat[16] = `xform -q -worldSpace -matrix nc1`;
```

```
xform -m $mat[0] $mat[1] $mat[2] $mat[3] $mat[4] $mat[5] $mat[6] $mat[7]
$mat[8] $mat[9] $mat[10] $mat[11] $mat[12] $mat[13] $mat[14] $mat[15] nc2;
```

Although the xform command is the caboose of the command documentation, it packs quite a punch. In short, it allows for polling and setting any of a node's transformation attributes, which means you can translate, rotate, and scale objects as well as center their pivots and zero out their transforms. In addition, you can use xform to get the bounding box of an object.

ANIMATION RETARGETING

Maya 6.0 now allows for retargeting of animation data from the joints of one skeleton to the joints of another skeleton. The source skeleton is the one that carries the data that you want to retarget the animation from, and the target skeleton is the one you want receiving the retargeted data. Retargeting animation is a great tool for transferring animation from one skeleton to another regardless of skeleton proportions. First, you must begin by setting up the source and target skeleton, with a neutral pose. The next step is labeling the joints of your source and target skeletons, by using the Skeleton, Retargeting, Joint Labeling menu to automatically label each joint in a selected joint chain, or you can relabel them manually through the Attribute Editor, just as long as they are labeled identically for both. After you have relabeled the joints, select the root of the first skeleton (source), and then the root of the second (target). Next, retarget the animation by navigating under the Animation menu to Skeleton, Retargeting, Toggle Selected Labels. The animation on the source skeleton should have been retargeted to the target skeleton.

HISTORY IS ONLY SKIN DEEP

Setting up a smooth bind skin character model can get pretty sluggish, especially if it's a very complex model. Odds are, there is a fair amount of history on that model, and every time you make a change the model has to update that history. A new feature to version 6.0 is the Delete Non-Skin History in the Animation menu under Skin, Edit Smooth Skin, Delete Non-Skin History. With the new Delete Non-Skin History option, you can now delete the history from your geometry and still retain all its smooth bind skin history.

   DEFORM POINTS OUTSIDE THE DEFORMER

It used to be that when you worked with lattice deformers you only had control over the points that were inside the lattice. Maya version 6.0 now gives you full control of those pesky points, by allowing you to choose from the method of influence within the lattice options menu. In the animation menu, navigate to Deform, Create Lattice, Options. In the options menu a new pull-down menu has been added to allow you to choose between three different methods of influence over the Outside Lattice deformer.

LATTICE DEFORM YOUR GRAPH EDITOR

Animators are the biggest control freaks in the CG biz. They want endless custom sliders and ways to manipulate their performances. Now in version 6.0 they can manipulate their curves in a number of new ways within the Graph Editor, the most interesting being the addition of the Lattice Deform Keys tool. Start by loading in some heavy curves, picking the keys, and then double-clicking the Lattice Deform Keys button just after the Add Keys button. You are presented with controls of rows and columns, which bind over the extents of the selected keys. Use your left mouse button to pick points, perhaps Shift-clicking additional ones, and then move them with the middle mouse button. What is next—fully, globally illuminated tube renders of curves? Hmm....

54

COLOR YOUR ANIM CURVES

In the quest to endlessly customize every nook and cranny of Maya, version 6.0 users can now apply custom colors to animation curves in the Graph Editor. Actually, more useful than just plain neurotic or obsessive behavior, this allows easy reading or filtering of dense motion-capture data, for example. Even more interesting is the ability to use MEL to add custom coloration to groups of curves linked to specific characters. This new control is not obvious, however, so start by selecting a curve, and then choose Graph Editor, Curves, Spreadsheet. By sliding down, you will find Use Curve Color, and an associated Color Editor. Bear in mind that only 20 custom colors are available, with the other 16,780,000 used for other things.

Dangerous
Effects
Animation

Effects animation is the real underdog of visual effects work. When done skillfully, it is invisible to the viewer because the willing suspension of disbelief kicks in (hopefully), and the viewer believes he or she is simply viewing natural phenomena, as opposed to the reality of an agonizingly worked-out and tediously orchestrated CGI effect. Effects artists spend their lives working hard at having complex events appear natural instead of man-made.

Dangerous Effects Animation

things you can do at home

Contributions by Eric Pender and Kenneth Ibrahim

It is diametrically opposed to character work, where the performance is highly intentional and demands your attention. Both forms of animation seek to create compelling cinematic performances. Character animation strives for emotional response, whereas effects animation strives for a visceral response. The pod race explosions in Star Wars Episode 1 *or the dramatic plane crashes in* Pearl Harbor *remain landmarks in arresting film experiences. Coincidentally, both of these were created primarily with the help of Maya dynamics. Known as a powerhouse for dynamics and particle work, Maya enables extremely robust re-creations of complex events. Even more powerful tools are now available in version 6.0, such as Particle Deformers, Per Particle Field Attributes, and Interactive Playback. Similar to character animation, effects animation remains as one of the deeper areas in the package to master, requiring patience and a cast-iron stomach for technical issues and minutia. These tips can be considered virtual antacids for the technical heartburn you may encounter along the way, and they also illustrate the depth and range of what is possible in Maya.*

DYNAMIC WINDOW LAYOUTS

Often you find yourself doing effects in between other tasks. It is often helpful to save a layout specifically for animating dynamically. Under Panels, Layout, select the Two Panes Side by Side layout. In the left pane, select Panels, Panel, Dynamic Relationships. This is like the Outliner window but enables you to connect and disconnect fields. To save the layout, select Panels, Saved Layouts, Edit Layouts, click the New Layout button, and finally change the name to something like Dynamics. Now, when you want to do some dynamic animation, select this layout to make the process easier.

USE PLAYBLASTING TO CHECK MOTION

Many times with dynamic animation, it is easy to get fooled by the speed of the default timeline playback. It is simply not real time when you play the simulation according to the speed of the graphics card, even though card speeds today are formidable. As soon as you feel your animation is reasonable, it is best to check it with playblasting. In the main menu, choose Window, Playblast option box. Set your desired frame range, select Fcheck, make a guess at display size based on available RAM, and then press Playblast at the bottom. This will do a sequential hardware capture of the selected viewport and then play it back in Fcheck. In Fcheck, press "T" to play back in real time mode. Often your perception of your animation will be much different at the correct speed. Also remember to set Playback Every Frame in the Playback section of Animation Preferences to ensure proper simulation.

A ONE-MINUTE OCEAN

You can now quickly create animated water. This used to be a very complicated task. Select the option box of Fluid Effects, Ocean, Create Ocean, choose Create Preview Plane, and complete with Create Ocean. Now add a Directional light pointing down. When you play the scene, the preview plane will move, and you can get a rough idea of the default motion. Change the values in the Ocean shader and render.

SOFT BODY ROPE TRICKS

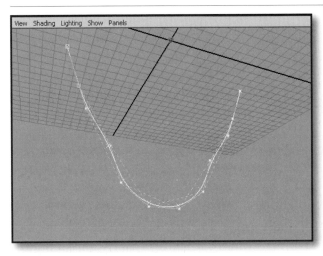

Rather than referring to the antics of an out-of-shape cowboy, this is actually a cool trick for animating a dynamic rope behavior. Make sure your grid is displayed and press the Snap to Grids option in the Status Line. Use the Create, EP Curve Tool to create a curve that is perfectly straight with each point on a neighboring point on the grid. Start on the left and click to the right one grid point over for an arbitrary ten units. Select the curve and from the menu choose the option box of Soft/Rigid Bodies, Create Soft Body. Under Creation Options, choose Duplicate, Make Original Soft. Click on Hide Non-Soft and Make Non-Soft a Goal. Set the weight to 1 and click Create. In the Status Line, press Select by Component Type and then select all the points in the curve except the two at either end. Press Ctrl-A to open the Attribute Editor and under the heading Per Particle Attributes, right-click in goalPP and select Component Editor. Select the Particles tab at the top, listing all selected points. Expand the window so that you see all the goalPP attributes. Click and drag from the top value to the bottom value of goalPP, press 0, and press Enter. All the selected points will now have a goalPP of 0, while the endpoints that we did not select will retain a value of 1. Close the window and then in the Status Line press the Select by Object Type button and select our original curve. In the menu, select Fields, Gravity. Reselect the curve and in the menu select the option box for Soft/Rigid Bodies, Create Springs. Change the Creation Method to Wireframe, the Wire Walk Length to 2, the stiffness to 10, and then press Create. Play the scene, and you can see how fun soft bodies can be. Experiment with spring stiffness and damping. Do a playblast to see it in real time.

ALL SOFT BODIES MUST REST

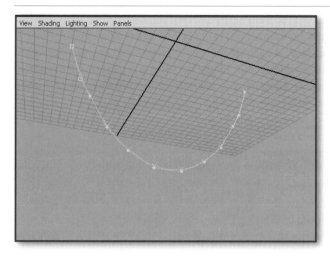

Let's now use the rope we made in the previous tip. Notice that it starts as a straight line and then falls and bounces around. As cool as that is, sometimes we want to do an animation that requires the soft body to start in a resting position. One way to get there is to set your frame range really high and play the scene until the object stops bouncing. Unfortunately, our particles have nothing to slow them down, so that can take a while, but there is a better way. Select the rope and then add Fields, Drag options. Set the Magnitude to 1 and the Attenuation to 0. By playing the scene, the rope will fall and then come to a rest rather quickly. Now, with the rope selected, choose Solvers, Initial State, Set for Selected. Rewind, and then play the scene, and you will find that the rope is not moving, being in a nice resting state. Disconnect the Drag Field from the rope by selecting the curve in the Dynamics Relationship Editor and on the right side with the Fields button checked, turn off the dragField1 by clicking once on it. Now save the file under a different name and add Rest to the end of it, for example. This technique is useful for anything that hangs, such as curtains. Start your animation from the rest state and then add wind and turbulence to get it moving.

JUMP THAT ROPE

In the previous tip, the goal object we originally created is called copyOfcurve1, to which the ends of the rope are attached. By containing the goalPP attribute of 1, it can still be really useful. So far we have simply used it to hold the rope still in space, but we may want the ends of the rope to move in space. Select the copyOfcurve1 and in the Channel Box, right-click in the Translation Z field and select Expressions. Enter this in the Expression field:

```
translateZ=8*sin(time*2);
translateY=8*sin(time*2);
```

Reconnect the drag field to our rope in the Dynamics Relationship Editor by selecting the original curve and then, on the right side, clicking on dragField1. Select dragField1, open its attributes, and change the Magnitude to .1. Make sure that your scene is set to play a lot of frames, perhaps up to 3000, and then hit play. The expression we put in the goal object will move the ends of the rope. Play the scene and let the motion develop. Now stop, rewind, and change the Stiffness setting of the springs to 20. Play the scene, and now the rope should work nicely after about 1000 frames. Notice how, when you change the stiffness of the springs, the reaction of the rope changes dramatically. Many times in dynamic animation, you need to experiment with the many variables to find the sweet spot.

A SIMPLE RIGID BODY ANIMATION

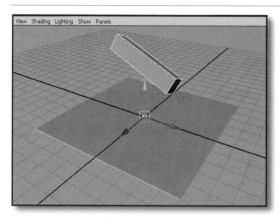

Often, learning a technique is a matter of experimenting with a very simple example and then applying what you have learned to larger examples down the road. Create a horizontal NURBS plane and scale it to 10 in all directions. Create a poly cube and raise it in Y 5 units. Select the NURBS plane and then select Soft/Rigid Bodies, Create Passive Rigid Body. Now select the cube and select Active Rigid Body. Next, with the cube still selected, choose Fields, Gravity. Play the scene, and you now have the most boring rigid animation possible. Rewind the scene, select the cube, and put a small amount of rotation on a few axes. Play the scene again and watch it get a lot more interesting. To adjust the way the floor or cube reacts, select the object, and then in the Channel Box you can change many variables such as Scale X to make a tube or Translate Y to add more height.

   ## A SIMPLE EXPRESSION TO MOVE A PASSIVE RIGID BODY

Using the same scene as the previous tip, let's modify it a bit with a powerful feature. In the Dynamics Relationship Editor, select the NURBS plane, right-click, and select Show Shapes. Click the cross next to the NURBS plane and then select rigidBody1. Press Delete, select the NURBS plane again, and then in the Channel Box, right-click in Translation Y and select Expressions. Enter this equation:

```
ty=.5*noise(time*3);
```

Press the Create button and then play the scene. The box will not hit the plane, but the plane will vibrate up and down. Now rewind, select the plane, and then make it a Passive Rigid Body again. Play the scene now, and you will see the box reacting to the movements of the plane.

USING PARTICLES TO VISUALIZE NOISE VERSUS RANDOM

When you are new to effects, one important concept to grasp is the noise field. Some people describe it as random, but it is actually not quite random. It is more based on a predictable natural randomness, which can look like clouds or mountains depending on how you use it. Here is a simple way to visualize the difference. Make a grid of particles with the Particles, Particle Tool options. Turn on Placement, With Text Fields, and then set the Minimum Corner to –10, 0, –10; the Maximum Corner to 10, 0, 10; and the Particle Spacing to .2. This will give you a plane of particles. Now select the Attribute Editor for the particles and under the Per Particle Attributes, right-click on Position and select Runtime Expression. Enter this:

```
position+=<<0,noise(position),0>>;
```

Play a single frame only by typing **2** in the current frame. Now you will see the particles raise or lower into a hilly pattern. Rewind the scene and replace the rule with:

```
position+=<<0,rand(1),0>>;
```

Now play one frame. Notice how the rand calculation is much more random while the noise is like periodic rolling hills.

RANDOMLY SIZED PARTICLES

To create more variation of particle sizes, we will begin by making a simple fountain. Create an emitter in Particles, Emitter options and choose Directional in Emitter type. Set the direction to 0, 1, 0 in Distance/Direction Attributes, the spread to .2, and the speed to 10. Now select particle1 and choose Fields, Gravity. In the particle1 Attribute Editor, go to Render Attributes, Particle Render Type and select Spheres. Now choose General under Add Dynamic Attributes, bringing up a window with several tabs at the top. Select the Particle tab, locate radiusPP, select it, and press OK. Now right-click in the field next to Per Particle (Array) Attributes, radiusPP and select Creation Expression. In the Expression Editor, enter:

```
radiusPP=.1+.5*rand(1);
```

Now upon playing this you will have created particles that receive a different radius based upon the equation we entered in the Creation Expression field. The function rand(1) returns a random value between 0 and 1.

BIGGER PARTICLES FALL FASTER

Now using what was created in the previous tip, let's make the larger particles fall faster than the small ones. In the particle1 Attribute Editor, right-click in the Per Particle (Array) Attributes acceleration field and select Runtime Expression. Enter this:

```
acceleration=10*<<0,-
particleShape1.radiusPP,0>>;
```

Before you play the scene, discon-nect the gravity field from the parti-cle in the Dynamic Relationships

Editor. Now the expression we entered in the Runtime rule controls how the particles fall. The smaller ones get very little gravity compared to the bigger ones. To enhance the scene further, adjust the equation to be:

```
acceleration=10*<<0,-particleShape1.radiusPP-.34,0>>;
```

PLAYBACK EVERY FRAME OR ELSE

Particle simulation requires run-up, a cache of calculations that enables successive frames to prop-erly compute. Normally this run-up is invisible to the user, but it does require that Play Every Frame is selected in Animation Preferences, Playback, Playback Speed. Odd behavior can be fixed by ensuring that this is set correctly; also remember to fully reset the playback to frame 0 before a new test.

MAKING PARTICLES COLLIDE WITH A FLOOR

Let's use the same animation as in the previous tip but add a floor. Create a horizontal NURBS plane and scale it up to 30 units. Play a few frames so that you see the particles and the new NURBS plane in the viewport. Select them both at the same time. Now, in the menu, select Particles, Make Collide. To verify that it was done, go to the Dynamics Relationships Editor, select particle1, and then in the right column, click on SELECTION MODES, Collisions. You should see nurbsPlaneShape1 listed. It should also be highlighted, which tells you that the current particle will collide with this object. Now play the scene, but chances are, you have a problem. Your emitter, located at 0, 0, 0, is on the plane, so some particles get emitted up and others bounce down. A simple solution is to raise the emitter in Y until all the particles start above the plane. To change the behavior of the collision, select nurbsPlane1 and open the Attribute Editor. Select the tab called geoConnector1, ignore the Tesselation Factor, and adjust the Resilience that influences the bounce, as well as the friction that controls how slippery the plane is.

   PARTICLE LOOPING

Often, particle effects can be useful to cycle repeatedly in order to create mapped 2D card replacements or rhythmic effects. In order to create a seam to provide temporal matching, select your particles on the last frame of the sequence and choose Solvers, Initial State, Set for Selected. Now the first and last frames will match, enabling seamless loops.

KILL PARTICLES WHEN THEY GO BELOW A CERTAIN HEIGHT

Continuing to build on the previous tip, let's kill the particles instead of colliding them. There can be many instances where you simply need to get rid of the particles instead of making them bounce. Fewer particles mean better performance, so getting rid of obscured particles will speed things up. Delete the plane that has the collision on it, open the Attribute Editor for particle1, and go to the Lifespan

Attributes, selecting lifespanPP only in Lifespan Mode. Now in the Per Particle Array Attributes, right-click in the lifespanPP and select Runtime Expression. Add the following lines to the existing line of code:

```
$pos=particleShape1.position;
if ($pos.y<0)
particleShape1.lifespanPP=0;
```

Click on Edit and Close and then play the scene. Now when the particles fall below 0, they die. Be sure to keep the emitter placed above 0 in Y because that would restrict emission.

WORKING ON THE CHAIN GANG

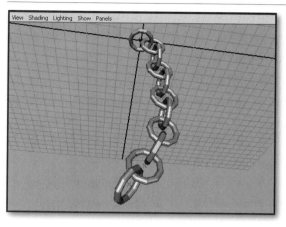

Helpful for rendering the latest rapper fashion accessories, here is an unusual use for rigid bodies. Start by choosing the option box for Create, Polygon Primitives, Torus. Change the Section Radius to .2 and the Subdivisions Around Axis and Height to 10. Make sure the radius is at 1, the twist is at 0, and the Axis is Y, and then press Create. Now, with pTorus1 selected, select the option box for Edit, Duplicate. Set the Number of Copies to 10 and make sure all options are unselected except for Copy and Parent. In the Translate box, enter 1.25, 0, 0 and in the Rotate box, enter 90, 0, 0. Make sure Scale is 1 and press Duplicate. Now only select the original pTorus1 and choose Soft/Rigid Bodies, Create Passive Rigid Body. Now select all the other ones and choose Soft/Rigid Bodies, Active Rigid Bodies. While they are still selected, choose Fields, Gravity. Now play the scene, and you have a dangling chain.

   BATTLE TWO TURBULENCE FIELDS TOGETHER

To really get rich and subtle effects with turbulence fields, use two of them with almost identical settings but slightly different frequencies and magnitudes. Then put opposite expressions in the Phase Field Attributes. For starters, try `phaseY=time*3` in one turbulence field and `phaseY=time*-3.3`. This will cause the fields to interact and give you cool motion that you otherwise could not get with a single field.

CHAPTER 8 • Dangerous Effects Animation   **213**

SWARMING BUGS OR ATTACHING FIELDS TO INDIVIDUAL PARTICLES

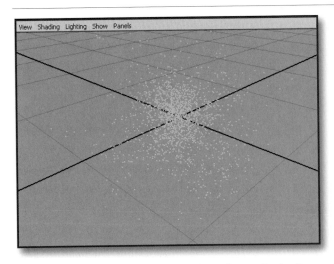

For your next massive bug attack movie, try this tip. Under the Particles menu, select Create Emitter options. Change it to an Omni with Speed set to 0 and Max Distance set to 1. Play the scene for 30 to 40 frames, but notice that there are particles emitted that are not moving at all. At this point, we want to freeze these particles in time and disconnect the emission. Select particle1 and then select Solvers, Initial State, Set for Selected. Next, in the Dynamics Relationships Editor, disconnect the emission. Do this by selecting particle1, and then, on the top right, select Emitters and click on emitter1 so that it becomes unhighlighted. Now when you rewind and play the scene, nothing happens, and the particles are idle. Select particle1 and then select Fields, Newton. Select both particle1 and newtonField1 and choose Fields, Use Selected as Source of Field. Now the field will be attached to each individual particle. In the newtonField1 Attribute Editor, select Apply Per Vertex under Special Effects. Now set the Magnitude to .1 and Attenuation to 0 under Newton Field Attributes. Last, make sure that Use Max Distance is unchecked. Set your timeline to be around 1000, hit play, and grab the bug repellant—you will need it.

MAKE A PARTICLE EMIT A TRAIL OF PARTICLES

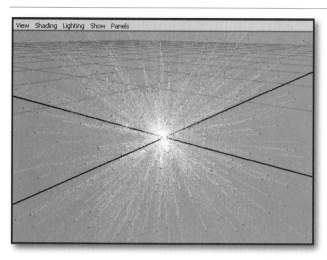

Let's use the bug swarm in the previous tip for this trick. Select particle1 to which we applied Newton Fields and choose the Particles, Emit from Object option box. Specify an Omni Emitter Type and press Create. Now if you play the scene, you will have particles all over that are not showing any trailing action. Select emitter2 that we just created and set the Speed to .1 under Attribute Editor, Basic Emission Speed Attributes. Next, choose particle2 and set the Lifespan Mode to Constant and the Lifespan value to .3 in its Attribute Editor. Next, go to the Add Dynamic Attributes section, select Opacity, and choose Add Per Particle Attribute. Right-click in opacityPP under Per Particle (Array) Attributes, choosing Create Ramp. Now right-click again in this field and select Edit Array Mapper. Change the Max Value from 1 to .2. Now change focus to the particleShape2 main attributes and under the Render Attributes, press the button that says Current Render Type and then change the Point Size to 1. Play the scene and experiment with different lifespans or add color with Add Dynamic Attributes, Color, Add Per Object Attributes for some cool effects.

EMIT PARTICLES FROM AN IMAGE OR TEXTURE

Here is a cool tip for either surreal or practical uses. Create a horizontal NURBS plane and scale it to 30. With nurbsPlane1 selected, choose Particles, Emit from Object options. Change the emission type to be Surface. Select emitter1 and press Ctrl-A to get the Attribute Editor. Scroll down near the bottom to the area titled Texture Emission Attributes. Under the Texture Rate slider, press the radio button titled Enable Texture Rate. Next, press the button to the right of the Texture Rate slider. This will bring up the Create Render Node window that will enable you to choose what texture to use. For a quick check to see whether it is working, select the Checker pattern. Now particles will only emit from where the checker pattern is not black. In the emitter1 attributes, turn the Speed to 0 and then play the scene. You will see a checker pattern appear slowly with the particles. Turn up the amount of parti- cles emitted to see the pattern better. To change the pattern, go into the attributes for the emitter, right-click on the Texture Rate attribute, and select Break Connection. Now you can add a different texture where the creative possibilities are quite endless, such as using an animated image map sequence.

KNOW YOUR FIELD OPTIONS

As you use dynamics increasingly, you may find you like to use certain settings as starting points. It is useful to set up fields initially so that basic setup work can be avoided. Many of these settings are common to all fields and work the same regardless of the field. Here are the common ones: Magnitude is the strength of a field or how hard it pushes a particle. This setting depends on the scale of your scene, but it's useful to set this to 1 typically. Attenuation tones down the magnitude of a field with distance, similar to light decays. Setting this to 0 means that the field will affect the particles regardless of how near or far they are from the field. As you increase this value, the effect is localized around the field. Values from 1 to 2 are best, but you should start with 0. Also it is helpful to turn Max Distance off. Now as you create a field with these settings, you will have a good starting point. Disabling Max Distance and Attenuation will reduce potential confusion when you first add a field.

   GET YOUR TURBULENCE ON

Adding a turbulence field to particles can create interesting and rich behaviors. Unfortunately, by default the turbulence pattern stays in place. Adding a simple expression on the Phase Y attribute will take care of this. Try `phaseY=time*3` as a starting point. You will now see the pattern of the turbulence move with time. You can move the turbulence any direction you want using Phase X and Phase Z in combination with Phase Y. Often it is preferable to move the phase away or toward the camera if possible.

EMIT MORE PARTICLES AS THE EMITTER GOES FASTER

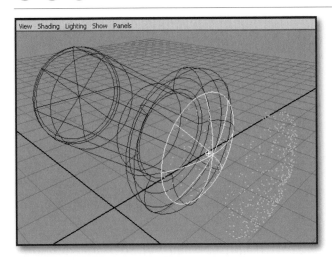

Here is a fairly advanced trick for which you may find a use. Maya typically does not let you vary emission rates with velocity, but this will enable such an effect. Create a sphere and add an expression to its translationX attribute, `tx=sin(time*3)`. As the scene is played, the ball should oscillate back and forth smoothly along X. With the ball selected, choose Particles, Emit from Object options, setting it as a Surface Emitter Type, setting the Rate (Particles/Sec) to 2000, and turning the speed to 0. In the particle1 Attribute Editor, turn Inherit Factor to 1 under Emission Attributes. Now under Lifespan Attributes, select lifespanPP only. Go down to the Per Particle (Array) Attributes, right-click on lifespanPP, and select Runtime Expression. Enter this expression:

```
$magv=mag(velocity);
if (rand(1)<linstep(0,1,$magv/3))
lifespanPP=1;
else
lifespanPP=0;
```

Now when you play the scene, you will see that the emission happens a lot more when the object is moving quickly. As the object slows down, very little emission takes place. To apply this to any other scene, you will need to know how fast the cutoff velocity is. To change that, change the numeral 3 under $magv/3 to another integer value. The trick only works because Maya lets us see the inherited velocity in the Creation Expression. Perfect for salt-shaker or ketchup bottle animation!

PARTICLE REPLACEMENT

Here's an excellent part of the dynamics package that can really help with flocking movement of large groups of objects—particle geometry instancing. Basically a way to lynchpin instanced copies of objects to each particle, it is a great way to do flocks of birds, basic crowds, or falling boulders. The source object can be animated, or it can be a sequence of objects. Per-particle attributes can enable individual modification of behavior, and different objects can be instanced to different particles. With a bit of ingenuity, many possibilities exist for complex animation when combined with the already rich particle toolset. To get started, create a simple primitive of your choice or hierarchical model if you like. Next, create a particle array with Particles, Particle Tool options set with Create Particle Grid checked, With Text Fields checked, and Minimum Corner set to –5, 0, –5 and Maximum Corner set to 5, 0, 5. After the particle array is created, select the object first, Ctrl-click to add the particle, and then choose Particles, Instancer (Replacement). Instance copies will now appear in place over each particle. Now, to make it interesting, apply some fields to the particle, such as Air, Gravity, and Turbulence. Playback will be sluggish, so plan on playblasting frequently to evaluate the animation. Many creative options exist in the Instancer options menu, so delve in with fervor!

INVASION OF THE BLOB

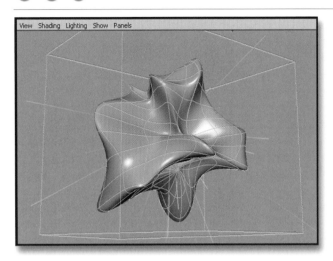

Soft bodies are one of the really fun and powerful features in Maya. A very simple but graphic demonstration of what they can do is an homage to the sci-fi classic *The Blob*. Start by creating a NURBS sphere with 16 spans and sections. Press "F" to fit the view. Right-click on the sphere and choose Materials, Assign New Material, Blinn. Change the color to .64, .80, .83 in RGB. Select the sphere and press 3 to increase screen resolution. In the dynamics menu, choose Soft/Rigid Bodies, Create Soft Body options and set Creation Options to Duplicate, Make Copy Soft, Hide Non-Soft Object, Make Non-Soft a Goal, and Weight of .7. Now go to Particles, Create Emitter options and set Type to Omni, Rate to 12, and Speed to 4. Open the particle1 Attribute Editor and set Render Attributes, Particle Render Type to Streak, Lifespan Mode to Constant with a Lifespan of .5 and Inherit Factor of 0. Set frame range to 100 and check for particle emission. Now with nothing selected, choose Fields, Air with settings of Magnitude 10, Speed 1, Direction XYZ all to 0, and Maximum Distance to 1. Now with airField1 and particle1 both selected, choose Fields, Use Selected As Source of Field. Open the Dynamic Relationships Editor and connect copyOfnurbsSphere1Particle to airField1. Now hit play and open the Attribute Editor for copyOfnurbsSphere1Particle. Nothing much happens until the Goal Weight for nurbsSphereShape1 is reduced from the default of .7 down lower. Blobby animation should begin, with many effects possible by altering Goal Smoothness, Emission Speed, and AirField Attenuation. Send out the government troops when necessary.

CACHE AND CACHE AGAIN

Normally, playback or playblasting of particle simulations is sufficient, but if scrubbing, play-ing in reverse, or clicking to an individual frame in the timeline is desired, run-up calcula-tions can be output to disk or RAM cache. This can be used per object or scene-wise. For individual particle objects to be cached to RAM, select the particle node and choose Solvers, Memory Caching, Enable. Make sure Windows, Settings/Preferences, Preferences, Dynamics, Run Up to Current Time is turned off. Play back sequence to load to cache, and then when done with it, choose Solvers, Memory Caching, Delete. To write to disk, choose Solvers, Create Particle Disk Cache. This method utilizes the cache even if additional fields are added, so to disable it, choose Solvers, Edit Oversampling or Cache Settings and uncheck Particle Disk Cache, Use Particle Disk Cache. If all this seems too involved for rou-tine work, Maya offers easier run-up options in Window, Settings/Preferences, Preferences, Settings, Dynamics with Run Up to Current Time options. By disabling this command, dynamics will not be calculated if you need to scrub to check behavior of other non-dynamic animation. The Save Startup Cache option also helps by saving a run-up cache in your file, as opposed to on disk.

WHIRLING DERVISHES

Here's one of those fruitful mishaps that happened to turn into a great tip. One normally thinks of the particle instancing mechanism only as a way to instance geometry onto particle systems for things such as pieces of robots being blown apart or chunks of rock falling. But what is not obvious is that interesting effects can be achieved by instancing particle systems to other particle systems. Try creating an initial particle system using the Particles, Particle Tool menu by setting the Number of Particles to 100 and the Maximum Radius to 4. Click on the origin to create the particle cloud. Then create a second particle system using Particle, Create Emitter, setting both the emitter's rate and speed to 2. Select the two particle systems, initial particle cloud first, and use Particle, Instancer (Replacement) to create the instancer. Voila! Particles on particles. Now try animating the rotation in Y of the initial particle system and watch them all rotate. For an interesting artistic touch, set the Particle Render Type of the instanced particle system to Streak and set the Tail Size to something large like 20. You might also want to set the Line Width to 2. Then render a frame using the Hardware Render Buffer with Multi Pass Rendering checked on and Render Passes again set to something large like 25. Finally, set Motion Blur to a large number like 30 for some pretty cool rave-ready renders! If you want to render out a whole animation this way, you'll need to cache the particle system for the motion blur to work properly. This is also a chance to emphasize the utility of the Hardware Render Buffer, which is quite useful in production.

HOLY SMOKES!

This is a great technique to use when creating smoke and dust simulations. To make these effects as realistic as possible, the particles should linger quite a while, just as real smoke and dust do, while setting the particles to die off in clumps to open holes in the system over time. An easy way to visualize this is to have particles emit from a surface. You can now emit from polygon meshes in version 6.0, so create a polygon plane and scale it by 20 in all axes. Then perform the following steps:

- Select the plane and create an emitting particle system via the Particles, Emit from Object menu.

- Set the Emitter Type attribute to Surface.

- Keyframe the emitter's rate to create a large burst of particles over the first few frames of the timeline (set the Curve Type to Step).

- In the particleShape's attributes, set the Lifespan Mode to lifespanPP only.

- Click on Add Attributes For Current Render type and set the Point Size to 50.

- Click on General and add three scalar float attributes to the particle system's shape node called lsMin, lsMax, and clumpyness, and set them to 5, 15, and 0.5 respectively.

- Now right click on the lifespanPP attribute and create the expression that is the heart of this technique. The key is to control the lifespanPP attribute using the noise function. Add this expression to the particle system's creation rule:

```
lifespanPP = lsMin + (lsMax - lsMin) * (0.5 + 0.5 * noise(position *
clumpyness));
```

continues on next page

CHAPTER 8 • Dangerous Effects Animation　**223**

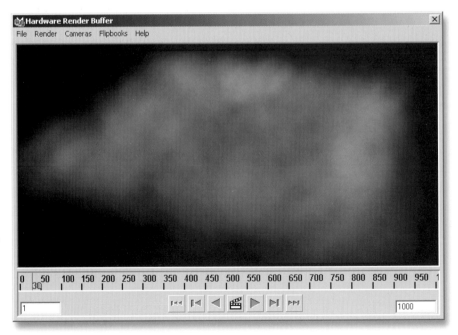

HOLY SMOKES! *(continued)*

First, notice that by having added your attributes to the particle system's shape node you don't need to qualify their names with the "." syntax when using them in the particle's creation expression. Maya will do that for you. Here's the rundown: Each particle's lifespan value starts with the minimum value, lsMin, and then has an additional amount added based on its birth position in noise space with a maximum value of lsMax. The scale of the noise space is controlled by the clumpyness attribute and determines how perceptually smooth or random the resultant particle cloud's breakup is over time. Finally, because the noise function returns values between -1 and 1, transpose it to the range 0–1 by first halving the value and then shifting it up by a half (0.5+0.5 *). To better visualize the lifespan values each particle receives, add the rgbPP attribute to the system by clicking on the Color button and selecting the Add Per Particle Attribute check box, and then add this line to the creation expression:

```
rgbPP = lifespanPP / lsMax;
```

The brighter the particle, the longer it lives. Try different values for the three attributes you added, especially the clumpyness value, which will reveal noise space itself! For the image, I changed the Particle Render Type to "Sprites" with a single smoke image mapped to all particles.

FADING IN AND FADING OUT

For particle effects such as the smoke described in the preceding tip, it's always best to modify the particle system's opacity both for added realism and to avoid the pesky "popping" behavior when particles are born. To control the opacity, add the opacityPP attribute using the Opacity button in the Attribute Editor. The opacity can then be controlled by an expression, but I find that this is one of those cases in which using a ramp is easier. To do so, right-click on the opacityPP line in the Attribute Editor and select Create Ramp. The ramp is grayscale by default. To avoid the popping issue, I add a color manipulator to the bottom of the ramp and make it black. The bottom of the ramp corresponds to the beginning of a particle's life and the top corresponds to its death. Likewise, black makes the particle transparent and white makes it completely opaque. I usually set the Interpolation type of the ramp to Bump or Smooth depending on the situation. It's often useful to use a combination of large quantities of particles with tiny opacity values. Sometimes the opacity values have to be so low that it's difficult to achieve the desired result using just the ramp editor. When you need more control you can navigate to the ramp's Array Mapper node by clicking on the Output Connections button from the ramp editor's page or by right-clicking over the opacityPP line in the particle shape's Attribute Editor page and selecting Edit Array Mapper. Once there, you can adjust the normalization of values for the ramp. For instance, you can effectively reduce all ramp values by half by setting the Max Value setting to 0.5.

RING OF FIRE

Another example of using the noise-based lifespan technique from the "Holy Smokes!" tip is a simple fire simulation. Create a NURBS circle and scale it by 10 in all axes. Create a particle system as described in the "Holy Smokes!" tip with the circle as the emitting geometry. Then, set the following:

- Emitter Type to Curve

- Rate to 5000 and Speed to 3

- DirectionX to 0 and DirectionY to 1

- Particle Render Type to MultiStreak

- Color Accum to on

- lsMin to 0, lsMax to 5, and clumpyness to 0.35

Now to give the ring of fire some variation and movement over time we'll do two things: First, add a scalar float attribute to the particle shape node called phaseMult and set it to 0.25; second, modify the creation expression as follows:

```
lifespanPP = lsMin + (lsMax - lsMin) * smoothstep(-0.5, 1, noise(position
* clumpyness + time * phaseMult));
```

The time * phaseMult component of the expression phase shifts the noise calculation, in essence moving the result through noise space over time. The smoothstep function is one of those you want to keep close, along with its brother linstep, in your arsenal of MEL artillery. Both functions normalize the third value in the range of the first two, linstep doing so linearly and smoothstep doing so quadratically. In this case, remap noise values between -0.5 and 1 to the range 0 to 1. Anything below the lower bound gets clamped to 0 and anything above the upper bound gets clamped to 1. By raising the lower bound you'll produce more 0 values resulting in more particle stillbirths (for lack of a better word), thinning out the production of flames. You may want to add these two bounds as attributes on the particle system as well. Last, give the flames some color by modifying the creation rule's rgbPP expression to the following:

```
rgbPP = <<1, 1, 0>>;
```

and add the following Runtime after Dynamics expression:

```
rgbPP = <<1, 1 - ageNormalized, 0>>;
```

This creates yellow particles at birth that turn red over the course of their lives. Try the same Hardware Render Buffer method mentioned in the "Whirling Dervishes" tip using a high number of render passes and lots of motion blur. Also try lengthening the tail sizes of the multiStreak particles in the Render Attributes section of the Attribute Editor as well as toggling on the Color Accum check box. You may want to add a turbulence field to the particles and set their Conserve attribute to around 0.97 to prevent the particles from getting out of control. Finally, try adding opacity to the particles as described in the "Fading In and Fading Out" tip.

INTERACTIVE PLAYBACK

For those times when you are fine-tuning dynamics and the way they behave, try Interactive Playback, a great new tool introduced to version 6.0. Interactive Playback enables you to adjust attributes interactively while the simulation loops in real time. For example, create a plane 20 units by 20 units, which will act as your ground plane. Now, create a cylinder with eight sides and a radius of 0.2 and duplicate it three or four times while randomly offsetting them from each other. Be sure the cylinders are floating above the ground plane. Next, make the plane a Passive Rigid Body object, and add a gravity field that only affects the cylinders. When that's all done and ready, enable Solvers, Interactive Playback and try changing some attributes from each of the cylinder objects. You see them react differently from one another right before your eyes.

PARTICLE DEFORMATION

Trying to shape particle behavior isn't always a straightforward task, and the more tools available to help ease this process along the better. In version 6.0, the ability to shape particle behavior is possible. Particles can now be affected by all deformers except for the skinning and blend shapes deformers. To deform particles, create a scene with particles and then select the particle object. In the Animation menu, click Deform and select the deformer you want to use on the selected particle object.

USING NUMERIC DISPLAY MODE

When particles don't seem to behave the way you'd expect, it's often reflected in the values of their per-particle attributes. A simple and convenient way to check these attribute values is to change the particle shape's Particle Render Type to Numeric. By default each particle is displayed as a number representing its id attribute, but any other attribute can be displayed instead by clicking the Current Render Type button next to the Add Attributes For label. This produces the Attribute Name field in which you can type the name of the attribute whose value you'd like to display. Try typing age. You should see scalar values that increase as you play back the animation indicating the ages of the particles. Try typing velocity. You should now see triple values at each particle position reporting each particle's velocity. This mechanism helps to debug particle states and errors in per-particle expressions and can save you lots of time and headache.

BIRTHING PARTICLES INTO NOISE SPACE

Interesting effects can be created by birthing particles based on noise space. The idea here is to kill particles that are born into regions of noise space with values less than some threshold and to leave the rest alive. To demonstrate, create an emitter with the following settings:

```
Emitter Type = Volume
Rate = 100000
Volume Shape = Sphere
Away from Center = 0.0
```

Scale the emitter up to about 10. Then, set the particle system's render type to Sphere, its Lifespan Mode to lifespanPP only, and add the following expression to the Creation rule:

```
float $freq = 0.35;
float $cut = 0.5;
lifespanPP = (noise(pos * $freq) > $cut) ? 100 : 0;
```

The $freq variable determines the size of the noise space and the $cut variable sets the threshold under which you can kill particles by setting their lifespans to 0. Play the animation and let the volume fill up a bit. Is anyone thinking grapes?! Now retire to a glass of wine and a good book.

CREEPY CRAWLY PARTICLES

Using particle goal weighting and a few specific per-particle attributes, particles can be made to crawl over a surface or mesh. The U and V values of the geometry are at the base of the effect so it's important that they are set as expected. Here's the crawler formula starting with a poly torus:

- Create a poly torus and scale it up as desired.

- Emit particles from the torus using Particles, Emit from Object menu.

- Make the torus a goal object using Particles, Goal menu.

- Change the emitter type to Surface.

- Check on the Need Parent UV option.

Next set the torus' Goal Weight to 1 in the particle shape node's Goal Weights and Objects frame and add the following attributes to the particle system from the Particle tab in the Add Attribute window: parentU, parentV, goalU, goalV. That completes the setup. Now you create the expressions to get the particles crawling, which simply advances the particle's goal in either U or V in each frame. First, the Creation expression sticks the particles to their birth positions on the surface like so:

```
goalU = parentU;
goalV = parentV;
```

Then, the Runtime before Dynamics expression incrementally increases the goal position, here in U, to move the particles across the surface:

```
float $inc = 0.005;
goalU = (goalU + $inc) % 1;
```

The modulo operator (%) is used to cycle the goal value, allowing the particles to cross the U = 1 boundary and continue their journey; otherwise they would all come to a screeching halt at the border. The $inc variable determines the distance across the surface the particles move per frame—and therefore their speed. At this point all of the particles crawl at the same speed, but varying them is easily done with the following modified goal setting line:

```
goalU = (goalU + $inc * abs(noise(id))) % 1;
```

The noise function is used to alter each particle's speed based on its ID number. Also, the absolute value (abs) function is used to make sure no particle stops or moves backward.

CONSERVE YOURSELF!

Working with particles often involves the use of fields such as gravity and turbulence. These forces impart accelerations to the particles and before you know it, your particle system can get out of control. To keep particles from gaining too much velocity, the Conserve attribute can be turned down. As the name implies, this attribute controls the percentage conservation of velocity from frame to frame and a small change has a large effect. All of a sudden simulations that didn't seem to be working as expected become manageable and promising. As a quick example, create an emitter, increase the rate to 200, and add a turbulence field with the following setting changes:

```
Magnitude = 5.0
Attenuation = 0.0
Frequency = 0.4
Interpolation Type = Quadratic
```

Play back the animation and notice how the particles start off following the turbulence pattern but then drift off into space. Now, reduce the Conserve value on the particle shape node from 1 to 0.94 and see how an interesting pattern emerges. Hopefully you're saying "Cool!" at this point.

INTERPENETRATION?! WHAT DID I "COLLIDE" WITH?

If you're trying to simulate a group of neighboring objects being broken apart (for example, a sheet of glass or a brick wall) but are plagued by interpenetration errors, you can separate each object dynamically by assigning each one to a different collision layer. The collider object is then set up to affect all collision layers. The collision layer is an attribute of the rigidBody node and is set to 0 by default. Here's a script to iterate over all selected rigid body objects and to renumber their respective collisionLayer attributes sequentially.

```
string $rbs[] = `ls -sl`;
int $i;
for($i=0; $i<size($rbs); $i++)
        setAttr ($rbs[$i] + ".collisionLayer") $i;
```

Now none of the objects will collide with each other, but they won't collide with the collider object either. By setting the collider's collisionLayer attribute value to -1, you can force it to interact with all collision layers. That should do it!

DEACTIVATING PARTICLE COLLISIONS

If you have particles colliding with geometry in your scene, and you'd like to temporarily deactivate the collisions, you can set the Resilience parameter on the associated geoConnector node to -1. To reactivate, simply set it back to the previous positive value. This won't work, however, if you have a particle collision event defined for the particle system.

  ### RUNNING MULTIPLE RIGID BODY SIMULATIONS

Rigid body setups can take a while to create, and after you've put the time into getting the system working, you'll no doubt want to do a number of different takes either for yourself or to present to a supervisor. Though not immediately apparent via the interface, Maya's handling of baked rigid body simulations provides a mechanism to record and switch between multiple bakings, a sort of caching system if you will. When a simulation is first baked, animation curves are created and assigned to the rigid body objects, replacing the real-time calculated results from the solver. For each of these channels a choice node is added between the animation curve and the geometry, allowing for the geometry to be driven by the curve or the rigid body solver based on the value of the Selector attribute of the choice node. Additionally, a new curve determining which index is current is created and piped into the rigidBody node's Baked Simulation Index attribute, which in turn is connected to the above-mentioned Selector attribute. You can trace all of this in the Hypergraph window, but what it boils down to is the fact that you can change which baked simulation to play back by manipulating this index curve. It's a 2-keyframe step-type curve whose first keyframe is the number of the current bake and whose second keyframe is set to -1, which represents the solver. So, after baking the first simulation, you can have the solver become active again by setting this index curve's first keyframe value to -1. Make any changes you like and bake again. This curve will now have an initial keyframe value of 2, indicating that baked simulation number 2 is current. Again, you can set the value to -1 and run another simulation. You can do this any number of times.

To play back a previous simulation, set the curve's initial keyframe value to the index number of choice. An easy way to access all of these index curves is to select the rigid bodies, display the Graph Editor and select the Driven by Anim Curve option in the Show, Attributes menu. Frame the curves, which are all overlapping, select the first keyframe, and set as desired. Play back the animation to confirm the choice.

ROW, ROW, ROW YOUR SIM GENTLY DOWN NUMBER STREAMS

New to version 6.0 is the provision of multiple random number streams, which come in handy for such things as repeated particle behavior. If the particle simulation requires, for instance, that each particle's mass attribute receive a unique value, the particle system can be set up to use a particular random number stream. This ensures that each particle's mass will be assigned the same value every time the simulation is played back, provided that you seed the stream at the beginning of each playback. When there was only one default stream, it was rather taboo to use the rand function, as there was no guarantee of repeatability when working on communal scene files in a production environment. Who knows who else might have been calling the rand function in an expression and throwing your expected values out of order. The noise function could be used instead with some multiple of the frame value as the argument to imitate a repeated random number sequence. Now random number streams can be associated with a name and everybody can agree to use different names for their respective streams. To see how this works, create a volume emitter and scale the default cube up in X and Z and down in Y to make it fairly flat. Set the emitter's rate to a low number like 10 and set the render type to numeric, specifying mass as the attribute name. Edit the creation rule to read as follows:

```
mass = rand("test", 0, 10);
```

The first argument specifies the stream name whose values you'd like to use. This string can be any name you like. If the stream doesn't yet exist, Maya will create it for you and seed it to return the default sequence of numbers in the range specified. If you play back the simulation now you'll notice that each time you rewind and play, different numbers are produced. These are the continuing numbers of the current stream. To repeat the sequence from the beginning on each playback, add the following non-particle expression:

```
if(frame == `playbackOptions -q -ast`)
    seed("test", 7);
```

This tells Maya to start the sequence from scratch if the current frame matches the beginning of the timeline. Different numbers can be passed to the seed function to produce different number sequences.

RENDERING HARDWARE-BASED PARTICLE TYPES IN SOFTWARE

If you need to render a particle system whose color is defined by the rgbPP per-particle attribute using Maya's software renderer, the particleSamplerInfo utility node comes to the rescue! Simply create a shader of your choice and assign a particleSamplerInfo node to its color channel by clicking on the checkered box next to the Color channel slider. In the Create Render Node window that pops up select the Utilities tab at the top, and then click the Particle Sampler button in the Particle Utilities frame at the bottom of the window. Next, assign the shader to the particle system with the rgbPP attribute and set the particle system's Particle Render Type setting to one of the software types such as Blobby Surface (s/w). Create a light in the scene and render away! In the example, I've created a surface-based emission system with the particles inheriting their color from the image mapped to the surface. I've also added a turbulence field to give the system some shape after birth and rendered with a threshold value on the blobbies, resulting in a kind of soupy rendition of the Maya startup screen. By default the particleSamplerInfo node knows about the basic per-particle attributes such as rgbPP and opacityPP and handles them for you, but it also allows for mapping of user-defined float and vector array per-particle attributes as well. This allows for some creative shading of particle systems.

Getting Under the Hood

Not to be confused with the cook at your local diner, MEL is the magic bullet in Maya. It is the ace in the hole, the *joie de vive*, the *raison d'etre for Maya's*

Getting Under the Hood
mud wrestling with MEL

Contributions by Erick Miller and Kenneth Ibrahim

existence. As for your existence, it makes life simultaneously easier and more difficult—it enables you to get under the hood and tweak to your heart's content, and it tempts you to spend endless hours doing so. The only catch is that there is a big bouncer at the door—the challenge of getting familiar with a programming language. Learning MEL in one chapter of an introductory book is not exactly a reasonable task, so this chapter will aim at those who are already underway in their exploration of the subject. If the bouncer doesn't seem too intimidating, it is certainly worth the time as the real unbridled power of Maya becomes yours. Unfortunately, only you will know of the massive powers you will wield, as your non-CG friends may not exactly see it that way.

HUH? USING *WHATIS* AND *HELP*

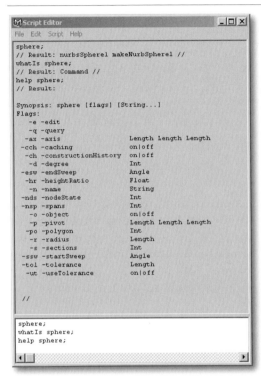

```
M Script Editor                          _ □ ×
File  Edit  Script  Help

sphere;
// Result: nurbsSphere1 makeNurbSphere1 //
whatIs sphere;
// Result: Command //
help sphere;
// Result:

Synopsis: sphere [flags] [String...]
Flags:
     -e -edit
     -q -query
    -ax -axis                 Length Length Length
   -cch -caching              on|off
    -ch -constructionHistory  on|off
     -d -degree               Int
   -esw -endSweep             Angle
    -hr -heightRatio          Float
     -n -name                 String
   -nds -nodeState            Int
   -nsp -spans                Int
     -o -object               on|off
     -p -pivot                Length Length Length
    -po -polygon              Int
     -r -radius               Length
     -s -sections             Int
   -ssw -startSweep           Angle
   -tol -tolerance            Length
    -ut -useTolerance         on|off


 //

sphere;
whatIs sphere;
help sphere;
```

When getting started with MEL scripting, you will have many questions running through your head. Besides constantly consulting the software manuals, there are a couple really useful MEL commands that were specifically designed to "help" users figure things out. First, the command whatIs can tell you exactly what any MEL-related thing is. If Maya can recognize it as either a variable, command, or MEL script that exists in its internal memory, then it will identify to you what it is. Let's start with a command that we can recognize: sphere. By typing the command `sphere` in the Script Editor, we can create a NURBS sphere. But what if we had not known what sphere was or what it did? How could we quickly and easily find out? Well, we could simply ask Maya to tell us by typing:

`whatIs sphere;`

Maya will happily tell us what it is: a command. Now that we know we're looking at a command, we can find out even more information by using the help command. Asking for help is simple. If we type `help sphere`, Maya will tell us all the information, including command-line flags and syntax, that it has registered about the usage of the sphere command. Note that the help command only works with commands and doesn't know about MEL keywords like if or while. Regardless, using whatIs and help can still be useful when trying to figure things out, especially during those times when you can use all the help you can get!

VARIABLES AND *EVAL* THIS, *EVAL* THAT

```
M Script Editor                               _ □ ×
File   Edit   Script   Help

string $arrayVariable[] = eval( "polyCube" );
// Result: pCube1 polyCube1 //
string $arrayVariable[] = `polyCube`;
// Result: pCube2 polyCube2 //

string $arrayVariable[] = eval( "polyCube" );

string $arrayVariable[] = `polyCube`;
```

Variables are, to put it simply, the places where you put data while your script is running. They are little storage cans into which you can stuff whatever you want dynamically. So, how do you get data from one location into a variable in your own MEL script? Well, first off, you only really need to know one simple thing—you "get" data by evaluating a procedure that "returns" the data into your variable. What, you may ask, is the data that is returned? Well, it doesn't matter what the data is. That's the whole point of having variables—they can contain pretty much anything you want. However, you do need to know that the data type of the variable does matter, and once you know that, you can start using variables to their full potential. Let's use the polyCube command as an example. The polyCube command makes a polygon cube and returns the names of the nodes that it made in a string array. If a command returns some data of a specific type, that means you can put it in a variable of matching type, just like this:

```
string $arrayVariable[]  = eval( "polyCube" );
```

Or, alternatively, back ticks will evaluate a command as well:

```
string $arrayVariable[]  = `polyCube`;
```

In either example, if you print the contents of $arrayVariable, you will get the array of names of the cube nodes that were created, pCube1 polyCube1.

CHAPTER 9 • Getting Under the Hood   **243**

ACTING CONDITIONALLY

Conditions are really just ways of making decisions based on a series of prerequisites. Sort of like a filter in your code, a conditional statement can keep certain things from happening and make other things happen instead if the condition tests true or false. There are a few different ways of writing a conditional statement, but the most common is by using the keywords if, else, and else if. Another cool way of writing a condition is by using a switch statement with case statements. The final, most cryptic but space-efficient way is by using the ? and : operators. The one thing to remember about conditions is this: A conditional statement is simply testing for true or false. This means that anything put into a condition must either evaluate to zero or one—and if it evaluates to one (in effect, true), then the condition tests as positive, and therefore that portion of code is executed. To be or not to be? Well, in a MEL script, it's based on the condition!

```
M Script Editor                                           _ □ X

File   Edit   Script   Help

;
THE CAR IS RED!
This vehicle has 4 wheels

string $vehicle = "car";
string $color = "red";
int $wheels = 4;

if( $vehicle == "car" )
{
      switch( $color )
      {
            case "red" :
                  print "THE CAR IS RED!\n";
                  break;
            case "blue" :
                  print "THE CAR IS BLUE!\n";
                  break;
            default:
                  print ("THE CAR IS "+$color+"!\n");
      }
}
else if( $vehicle == "truck" )
{
      print "THE VEHICLE IS A TRUCK!\n";
}
else
{
      print ("THE VEHICLE IS"+$vehicle+"\n!");
}

print (($wheels!=4) ? "This vehicle needs some repair\n" : "This vehicle has 4 wheels\n" );
```

THE SHEER EXCITEMENT OF ARRAY VARIABLES

```
M Script Editor                                    _ □ ×
File  Edit  Script  Help

  string $array[];
  $array[0] = "one";
  // Result: one //
  $array[1] = "two";
  // Result: two //
  $array[2] = "three";
  // Result: three //
  $array[ `size $array` - 1 ] = "four";
  // Result: four //
  clear( $array );
  // Result: 0 //

  string $array[];

  $array[0] = "one";
  $array[1] = "two";
  $array[2] = "three";
  $array[ `size $array` - 1 ] = "four";

  clear( $array );|

◄ |                                            ► |
```

Need to store a big list of stuff? Then an array is just right for you. Arrays are dynamically growing data structures in MEL; you can have arrays of many different data types—integers, floats, strings, and vectors. Unfortunately, you can't have an array of matrices, but that's probably all right. Using arrays is quite simple and can be very useful. Let's say you need to write a script that puts an unknown amount of string data into a list in order to keep track of things. Well, using an array to store everything is the thing to do. You can start using arrays by simply assigning data to each element in the list; for example:

```
string $array[ ];
$array[ 0]  =  "one";
$array[ 1]  =  "two";
$array[ 2]  =  "three";
```

You can then dynamically add new elements into the array by using the `size` command and indexing the array using the current size minus one, like this:

```
$array[ `size $array`-1]  =  "four";
```

One important thing to remember about arrays in MEL is that they are the only data type that is passed by reference—that means that if you pass an array into a MEL procedure, the procedure has the capability to directly modify the contents of the array that you just passed into it. This is so Maya does not have to make an entire copy of the array in memory just to pass the data around from one procedure to another. Finally, you can delete all the contents of your array by using the "clear" command. To completely destroy an array from memory, simply type:

```
clear( $array );
```

DOING THE LOOP

```
Script Editor                                    _ □ ×
File  Edit  Script  Help
int $intArray[] = { 0, 1, 2, 3, 4, 5, 6, 7, 8, 9, 10 };
for( $elem in $intArray )
{
        print ( "Array Element  " + $elem + "\n" );
}
;
Array Element   0
Array Element   1
Array Element   2
Array Element   3
Array Element   4
Array Element   5
Array Element   6
Array Element   7
Array Element   8
Array Element   9
Array Element   10

int $intArray[] = { 0, 1, 2, 3, 4, 5, 6, 7, 8, 9, 10 };
int $i = 0;
while( $i <= 5 )
{
        print ($intArray[$i]+ " is less than equal to 5...\n");
        $i++;
};
0 is less than equal to 5...
1 is less than equal to 5...
2 is less than equal to 5...
3 is less than equal to 5...
4 is less than equal to 5...
5 is less than equal to 5...
```

```
int $intArray[] = { 0, 1, 2, 3, 4, 5, 6, 7, 8, 9, 10 };
for( $elem in $intArray )
{
        print ( "Array Element  " + $elem + "\n" );
}

int $intArray[] = { 0, 1, 2, 3, 4, 5, 6, 7, 8, 9, 10 };
int $i = 0;
while( $i <= 5 )
{
        print ($intArray[$i]+ " is less than equal to 5...\n");
        $i++;
```

What is a loop? Well, it's not a dance, although it may feel like one when you are done! A loop is an extremely useful way of cycling over lists of data or building up lists of data. A loop is usually either a way to process the contents of an array or a way to repeatedly execute a set of commands in order to build an array. Sometimes, though, it is useful to execute a bunch of commands over and over again without returning data until a certain condition is met that tells us that it is okay to stop. There are two different keywords for writing loops in MEL, "for" and "while". Here is a simple example of using a "for" loop:

```
int $intArray[ ] = { 0, 1, 2,
➡3, 4, 5, 6, 7, 8, 9, 10 };
for( $elem in $intArray )
{
print ( "Array Element  " +
➡$elem + "\n" );
}
```

And here is an example of using a "while" loop:

```
int $intArray[ ] = { 0, 1, 2, 3, 4, 5, 6, 7, 8, 9, 10 };
int $i = 0;
while( $i <= 5 )
{
        print ($intArray[ $i] + "is less than 5...\n");
        $i++;
}
```

WRITING CUSTOM PROCEDURES

There comes a time in everyone's life when regular MEL just isn't enough, when custom logic is needed that MEL doesn't offer right out of the box. When that time comes, writing a custom procedure can answer all your needs. Writing a procedure in MEL enables you to define your own arguments, create your own block of logic, and then return the values that you have calculated as data that can be stored in other variables and used from within other scripts. If written generically and in enough of a multi-purpose fashion, sometimes your custom procedures can even be reused continuously by yourself or others. So, let's break down a custom procedure.

```
global proc string exampleProcedure( string $arg )
{
//
// any custom logic goes here:
string $variable = "The string I passed in is: "+$arg;
return ( $variable );
}
```

First, the keyword global tells Maya that what you are declaring should be available to the rest of Maya as a global function. Next, the keyword proc tells Maya that you are declaring a procedure. Next, the keyword string basically says that this procedure is going to return some data and is defining the data type that will be returned as a string. Next is the name of the procedure, which can be anything you like, and enclosed within parentheses are the arguments to the procedure—what the input must be for the procedure to run. Finally, within the brackets, known as scope operators, you can put whatever logic you want. When you are done writing your custom logic, all you need to do is return the answer using the return statement. Just make sure that the data type you are returning is the same type as what is declared at the beginning of the function. You can then use your custom procedure in another script by first making sure you source the script that contains the custom procedure and then doing something like the following:

```
string $fun = "this is fun";
string $value = 'exampleProcedure $fun';
```

OOPS: *WARNING, ERROR,* AND *CATCH*

```
Script Editor                                    _ □ ×
File  Edit  Script  Help
if( $badCondition == true ){
      error "An error has occurred.  Sorry, but something went wrong.";
};
// Error: An error has occurred.  Sorry, but something went wrong. //

int $badCondition = true;

if( $badCondition == true ){
      error "An error has occurred.  Sorry, but something went wrong.";
}
```

Sometimes planning for errors is just as much a part of the script writing process as writing the actual script. Adding additional code to handle certain cases that might cause errors is a process known as error handling. One really easy way to notify yourself that an error has occurred inside of your code before anything really bad happens is by using the MEL command error. The error command will immediately exit from your script and display a red error message in the Script Editor output. Creating an if statement that will be entered into when an error occurs is probably the most common way of using the error command:

```
if( $badCondition == true ){
        error "An error has occurred.  Sorry, but something went wrong.";
}
```

If you encounter a situation that's not an error, but there is still potential that a problem may occur, then try using the warning command. The warning command is similar to the error command in that it prints a colored message at the bottom of the screen to alert the user, but warning does not cause the script to fatally exit. Instead, warning continues to execute the rest of the script after it is called. We don't like errors and prefer Maya to continue generally, which is what the catch command is for. Anywhere in your code where you think you might encounter an error that isn't really an error is a good place to use the catch command. A good example of this would be deleting all cameras in your scene, but Maya gives you an error if you do that because it just won't let you delete the very last default camera. You could add extra logic to check for that, or you could simply wrap the delete command with a catch:

```
//
// FORCE DELETE ALL CAMERAS IN THE SCENE ->
//
string $cameras[] = 'ls -type camera'
for($cam in $cameras)
{
camera -e -sc false $cam;
}
catch('delete $cameras');
```

So, if you want your script to error out, use the error command; if you know there will be an error, and you want your script to keep on executing, then use the catch command.

USING CREATENODE, NODETYPE, AND LS

Pretty much everything that's useful in Maya is represented by a node. To list all the node types in Maya, you can print out the results from the ever-so-useful ls command:

```
print 'ls -nodeTypes';
```

You'll see that this yields a really long list. But say you need to create a node of a particular type in your script—*how do you do that*? It's simple: Use the createNode command and pass it the node type that you want to create:

```
createNode plusMinusAverage;
```

The preceding command creates a single math utility node of type plusMinusAverage. All node types that exist in Maya can be created this way and will be initialized in their default state. This is a useful thing to know because sometimes you don't want to jump through hoops just to create a simple node. Also, you might want to find out what the type of a node is that already exists in your scene. This is also a simple matter of calling a single command, called nodeType, and passing in the name of the node whose type you would like to query. Let's say we create a NURBS sphere from the Create menu. If we then want to find out what the type is for the NURBS shape node, we can call the following command:

```
nodeType nurbsSphereShape1;
// Result: nurbsSurface //
```

The text nurbsSphereShape1 is the name of the shape node of the sphere that we just created. The result of this command is a string that represents the node type; in this case, the result is nurbsSurface, which is the generic node type that represents all NURBS surfaces in Maya. So remember: If it is a node, then it has a corresponding type.

ADDING, GETTING, SETTING, AND CONNECTING ATTRIBUTES

Attributes in Maya can be incredibly useful as a general way either to store data or to pass data from one node to another. MEL exposes many ways to control attributes, from creating them to getting, setting, and connecting them. To create an attribute, use the MEL command addAttr. First, select an object that you want to add the attribute onto and execute this:

```
addAttr -ln myCustomAttribute -at double;
```

To set your newly created attribute's keyable property to true (so that it shows up in the Channel Box and can be keyframed), use the MEL command setAttr:

```
setAttr -e -keyable true .myCustomAttribute;
```

You can also use `setAttr` to set actual attribute values:

```
setAttr .myCustomAttribute 2.25;
```

If you need to get the value of an attribute, you can use the MEL command getAttr:

```
getAttr .myCustomAttribute;
// Result: 2.25 //
```

Finally, if you want to connect two attributes together so that your newly created attribute controls another attribute, you can use the connectAttr command:

```
connectAttr .myCustomAttribute .translateY;
```

Now the custom attribute that you created is controlling the translateY attribute of the transform node that it was added to.

ARRAY ATTRIBUTE OR ATTRIBUTE ARRAY?

You might think that you could easily create an array of string attributes on a node for storing a list of strings. Both beginning and experienced MEL scripters will find they instead need to have a string array attribute. After reading the MEL addAttr documentation, they will try to add an attribute that is of data type stringArray, like this:

```
addAttr -ln stringArrayAttribute -dataType stringArray;
```

Inevitably, they will be plagued with an error because the attribute is a complex data type, which is likely not what you want if having a simple array of strings that you can easily get and set from within MEL is your goal.

All attributes can be made into an array, regardless of their type, by using a single flag in the addAttr command! This means that Maya creates a distinction between the data types of attributes and the capability to create multiple elements as an attribute array. The option of calling an attribute a "multi" attribute is Maya's way of saying it can be expanded into an array of multiple attributes. After you make an attribute a multi, you can then refer to its elements by using the standard array index operators—for example, [0], [1], [2].... Here is an example of creating a multi attribute and then automatically expanding that attribute into an array using setAttr:

```
addAttr -ln myMultiString -dataType "string" -multi;
setAttr -type "string" .myMultiString[ 0]   "WOW!";
setAttr -type "string" .myMultiString[ 1]   "HERE IS";
setAttr -type "string" .myMultiString[ 2]   "AN EXPANDING";
setAttr -type "string" .myMultiString[ 3]   "ARRAY ATTR!";
```

It works with any attribute type you give it, including doubles, ints, and so on. The first attempted method doesn't work because the data of an attribute that is of data type stringArray is storing an entire array all in one attribute, not individually as separate elements. Because Maya has deemed these string array attribute data types as "complex" data, it does not yet have a mechanism in MEL for performing getAttr on them.

OBJECT DISPLAY JUGGLING

While working in Maya's modeling windows you often need to toggle the display of objects on and off to make it easier to work with the scene file. This is done using the Show menu at the top of any of the model panels. You are probably focusing on one task at a time and therefore choosing to display a distinct set of objects (i.e., NURBS Surfaces, Polygons, and Locators only), so you'll no doubt find yourself repeating these settings each time you change the panel layout. Here's a simple script to set the display of desired objects only, thus avoiding the need to access the Show menu repeated times per model panel.

```
string $wfPanel = `getPanel -wf`;
modelEditor -alo 0 -e -ns 1 -sds 1 -pm
1 -lt 1 -ca 1 $wfPanel;
```

The first line retrieves the panel that currently has focus and the second line instructs that panel what to display. This command tells it to show NURBS Surfaces, Polygons, Subdiv Surfaces, Lights, and Cameras. You can display different sets of objects by specifying different options to the modelEditor command. A quick way to view the available options is to use the help command as follows:

```
help modelEditor;
```

To make things even faster this script could be assigned to a Marking Menu, enabling you to set the display by a simple gesture over the window of interest.

IMAGE ON, IMAGE OFF

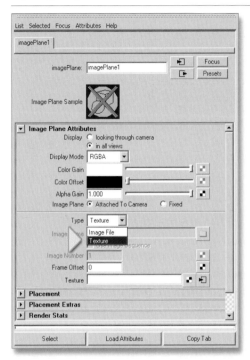

Working on shots in production often involves matching your work to a background plate. This background plate is usually made available to you in the form of a camera Image Plane. While it's necessary to have the Image Plane there, it tends to slow down playback dramatically depending on your available memory and machine configuration. You may have multiple Image Planes in the scene but for any given one, in this case imagePlane1, here's a script you can put on the shelf that toggles the display of the Image Plane on and off.

```
int $tgl = (`getAttr
imagePlane1.type` == 0) ? 1 : 0;
setAttr imagePlane1.type $tgl;
```

This actually switches the type of display of the Image Plane from "Image File" to "Texture," which ends up being a fast way to toggle its display in the modeling windows.

BIRDS OF A FEATHER CAN BE PROCESSED TOGETHER

MEL, like other programming languages, offers looping constructs, and like other scripting languages, offers the following form of the much-used for statement:

```
for($object in $objects)
```

This makes it easy to act on a number of objects that share some characteristic. For example, to iterate over the list of currently selected objects and turn their primary visibility off, you might use the following code snippet:

```
string $obj, $objs[] = `ls -sl`;
for($obj in $objs)
        if (`objExists ($obj + ".primaryVisibility")`)
                setAttr ($obj + ".primaryVisibility") 0;
```

Notice how it first checks to make sure that the object has the desired attribute, otherwise the code would fail when it encountered an object without it. (Another error-checking approach would be to use the catch command which is described in another tip in this chapter, "Oops: *Warning, Error*, and *Catch*.")

Another example would be to fish out non-referenced objects from a referenced group in order to delete them before being able to remove the reference group. This could be done as follows:

Select the referenced hierarchy.

Run select –hi to select all of the objects in the hierarchy.

Run the following code:

```
string $obj;
for($obj in `ls -sl`)
            if (!`reference -q -inr $obj`)
    delete $obj;
```

Notice how the ls command is embedded within the for construct, resulting in more compact code. Also, the reference command is being queried to provide you with the information you need.

Another technique is to use the ls command to filter out a group of objects on which to operate. Suppose that you're using RenderMan but have decided to rid your scene of all RenderMan-related subdivision nodes. You can first use the nodeType command on any one of these nodes to determine that its node type is mtorSubdivNode. Then you can delete them all with this code snippet:

```
select -r `ls -type mtorSubdivNode`;
delete;
```

Here the ls command is used with the –type option to identify all "mtorSubdivNodes" in the scene and is in turn wrapped in a call to the select command to create a selection list for deletion. By adding the –sl option to the ls call you could, for example, narrow the search to nodes of this type that are currently selected. Have a look through the ls documentation, and you'll find many useful options that can be mixed to produce the results you want. This combined use of the ls and select commands provides a powerful mechanism for parsing and operating on the contents of the scene file.

EXECUTEFOREACHOBJECT AND SELECTEDNODES

Some examples in the last tip demonstrated iterating over all selected nodes and performing some operation on them. Though the code to do this isn't by any means complicated,
MEL provides two convenient routines to help out. The first is the selectedNodes command,
which simply returns a string array containing, appropriately, all selected nodes. The second
is the executeForEachObject command, which allows you to specify an array of objects on
which to operate and an operation to perform on each of them. The command gives progress
feedback in the Script Editor window. Say that there is some geometry being deformed by a
lattice called "defLat" and you need to add additional geometry to it. Here's how you might
accomplish this given that you first select the geometry to add:

```
string $cmd = "lattice -e -g %s defLat";
string $itemList[] = selectedNodes();
string $results[] = executeForEachObject($itemList, $cmd);
```

The %s in the command definition will be replaced with the items in the list by the
executeForEachObject procedure.

```
Script Editor                                           _ □ X

File  Edit  Script  Help

string $cmd = "lattice -e -g %s defLat";
string $itemList[] = selectedNodes();

string $results[] = executeForEachObject($itemList, $cmd);
lattice -e -g "|nurbsSphere1" defLat;
lattice -e -g "|pCube1" defLat;
lattice -e -g "|pSphere1" defLat;
lattice -e -g "|nurbsTorus1" defLat;
lattice -e -g "|nurbsCylinder1" defLat;
lattice -e -g "|nurbsCone1" defLat;
// Result:   //

string $cmd = "lattice -e -g %s defLat";
string $itemList[] = selectedNodes();

string $results[] = executeForEachObject($itemList, $cmd);
```

HEY, BREAK IT UP!

```
Script Editor                                        _ □ ×
File  Edit  Script  Help
string $path, $paths[];
int $numPaths = tokenize(`getenv "MAYA_SCRIPT_PATH"`, ";", $paths);

print($paths);
F:/GRAPHICS/Maya/projects/Maya6KillerTips/mel
F:/GRAPHICS/Maya/6.0/scripts
F:/GRAPHICS/Maya/scripts
F:/GRAPHICS/Maya/6.0/presets
F:/GRAPHICS/Maya/6.0/prefs/shelves
F:/GRAPHICS/Maya/6.0/prefs/markingMenus
E:/Program Files/AliasWavefront/Maya6.0/scripts/startup
E:/Program Files/AliasWavefront/Maya6.0/scripts/others
E:/Program Files/AliasWavefront/Maya6.0/scripts/AETemplates
E:/Program Files/AliasWavefront/Maya6.0/scripts/paintEffects
E:/Program Files/AliasWavefront/Maya6.0/scripts/cloth
E:/Program Files/AliasWavefront/Maya6.0/scripts/live
E:/Program Files/AliasWavefront/Maya6.0/scripts/fur

string $path, $paths[];
int $numPaths = tokenize(`getenv "MAYA_SCRIPT_PATH"`, ";", $paths);

print($paths);
```

When doing things procedurally or programmatically in Maya, you are often required to convert a single string of data into a list of separate elements to process. This can be done easily using the tokenize command. It takes as arguments the original string to break up, the character with which to break it, and a string array in which to store the broken bits. It returns the number of bits broken. Let's say, for instance, that you'd like to get a list of all of the paths defined in the MAYA_SCRIPT_PATH environment variable and print out all of the files in each path. First you would retrieve the paths as follows:

```
string $path, $paths[];
int $numPaths = tokenize(`getenv "MAYA_SCRIPT_PATH"`, ":", $paths);
```

Using the getenv command will return the contents of the environment variable as a single string where each path is delimited by the ":" character on Unix-based systems and the ";" character on Windows. Use tokenize to break out all of the paths so that you can access them in the following code block:

```
string $file, $files[];
print("searching...\n");
for($path in $paths)
{
      print($path + "\n");
      $files = `getFileList -folder ($path + "/")`;
      for($file in $files)
            print("  " + $file + "\n");
}
print("done!\n");
```

The getFileList is another handy command that returns a list of files in the specified directory. The caveat here is that the path must end with "/". Also notice the formatting in the print statements. They create an organized listing in the Script Editor window.

FBM IN THE AM FOR A RENDER IN THE PM

Maya's noise function comes in handy in any number of situations, but to go the extra step you can implement Fractional Brownian Motion (FBM), which provides a more complex pattern. The noise function is layered a specified number of times, with the frequency being increased and the magnitude of the result being decreased with each layer. The frequency multiplier is commonly referred to as Lacunarity and is typically set to 2, which both doubles the frequency and is the reason the number of layers is referred to as Octaves (this, of course, is a musical reference where each Octave is a doubling in frequency or pitch). The magnitude of each pass is usually halved in value by a variable called Gain. You start with a base frequency and magnitude, which can be defined as variables in an expression to implement the FBM.

```
float $mag = 2.0;
float $freq = 0.1;
float $lacunarity = 2.0;
float $gain = 0.5;
int $i, $octaves = 10;
float $sum = 0.0;
for($i=0; $i<$octaves; $i++)
{
        $sum += $mag * noise(time * $freq);
        $freq *= $lacunarity;
        $mag *= $gain;
}
fbmLoc.translateY = $sum;
```

Here I've created a locator named fbmLoc and am mapping the FBM result to its translateY attribute. To see the complexity of the FBM expression, select the locator, open the Graph Editor and check on View, Show Results. Try different magnitude and frequency values and see what you get.

An option is to take the absolute value of the noise function, which results in what is commonly referred to as turbulence. Here's the modified line:

```
        $sum += $mag * abs(noise(time * $freq));
```

HOW FAR APART ARE THEY?

It's often handy to perform some operation based on the distance between two objects. As they approach each other, you may need to scale them or alter the value of some other attribute you've set up on the objects for shading and so on.

Here's a quick expression that calculates this distance:

```
// retrieve the positions of the 2 objects
vector $pos1V = `xform -q -ws -t object1`;
vector $pos2V = `xform -q -ws -t object2`;
// calculate the distance
float $dist = mag($pos2V - $pos1V);
// do something with the result
print($dist + "\n");
```

The xform command is used to fetch the translate values (-t) in world space (-ws) for each object. These results are stored directly into vectors for use with the mag command which is a convenient new bit of functionality in version 6. mag returns the magnitude of a vector, in this case the vector between the two objects, and thus the distance between them. You could calculate the distance manually by taking the square root of the sum of the squares of the differences in the x, y, and z components of the objects, but it's nice to take advantage of Maya's built-in vector functionality. You can now use other vector-based commands, such as unit, which would give you the direction between the objects. You could use this information, for instance, to have one object fire particles at the other.

YUM ENUM

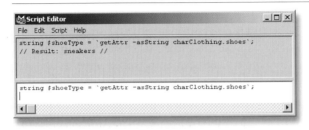

It used to be a problem that polling the value of an enum attribute would only return the index of the selected item after you'd spent all of that time typing in meaningful strings. Now you can get the string that the attribute's option menu is set to using the new –asString flag. For the charClothing node, each clothing descriptor enum attribute is set to a different index. Using this new flag on the shoes attribute, for instance, returns the string sneakers, as opposed to the number 3. Here's the command in all its splendor!

```
string $shoeType = `getAttr -asString "charClothing.shoes"`;
```

CLEAN UP THOSE DIRTY NODES

You may come across situations in which the scene file doesn't seem to be updated as you would expect. A surefire method to get Maya to update the scene and clean any dirty nodes is to run the dgdirty –a command. This is often employed after loading scenes with proprietary nodes to make sure everything is in order. All nodes in Maya accept data as input, perform some calculation, and provide the results as output. As new data appears on a node's inputs, the node is marked dirty by Maya and then re-evaluated to update its outputs. In this way, the entire scene graph is cleansed. The dgdirty command allows the user to manually set nodes to dirty for Maya to update and the –a option marks all nodes dirty, forcing Maya to re-evaluate everything.

EXPAND YOUR HORIZONS AND YOUR FILTER

To figure out which objects of certain types are currently selected, the filterExpand command is indispensable! It works to identify objects and components on the selection list via masks. If, for example, you need to know if any NURBS CVs are selected and warn the user of it before performing some operation, you would use the command with the CV mask as follows:

```
filterExpand -sm 28;
```

This will return a list of any CVs selected in a compact, or abbreviated, format. If you need the return results separated out as individual items, you can add the expand flag to the previous call, yielding the following:

```
filterExpand -ex true -sm 28;
```

The ls command will also return compacted lists as individual items in like fashion, with a gem of an option called "flatten." Try ls -sl -flatten.

```
Script Editor                                              _ |□| X|
File   Edit   Script   Help
filterExpand -ex false -sm 28;
// Result: nurbsSphere1.cv[5][1:2] nurbsSphere1.cv[5][5:6] nurbsSphere1.cv[6][0:7] /,
filterExpand -ex true -sm 28;
// Result: nurbsSphere1.cv[5][1] nurbsSphere1.cv[5][2] nurbsSphere1.cv[5][5] nurbsSphere1.cv
◄ |                                                              | ►
─────────────────────────────────────────────────────────────────
filterExpand -ex false -sm 28;

filterExpand -ex true -sm 28;
◄ | |                                                            | ►
```

TO BACKTICK OR NOT TO BACKTICK

It's really a question of style. MEL commands can be executed inline by surrounding the command with backtick (`) characters to catch their return value as follows:

```
string $objs[] = `ls -sl`;
if (!`size $objs`) print("nothing selected!\n");
```

In addition, MEL commands can be executed with the more familiar programming style of following the command name with its parameter list in parentheses. Using this syntax, the previous line would become:

```
if (!size($objs)) print("nothing selected!\n");
```

An advantage to using the more programming-esque style is that you can create multiple levels of command embedding. For instance, you can rewrite the previous statements into a single line as follows:

```
if (!size(`ls -sl`)) print("nothing selected!\n");
or even:
if (!size(ls("-sl"))) print("nothing selected!\n");
```

But the following will result in an error:

```
if (!`size `ls -sl``) print("nothing selected!\n");
as will:
if (!`size ls("-sl")`) print("nothing selected!\n");
```

When using the programming style syntax, simply place the command parameter options in double quotes and separate each parameter with a comma. So, to list all selected cameras (cameras whose shape nodes are selected) in the scene, the command would look like this:

```
ls("-sl", "-ca");
```

```
Script Editor                                                        _ |□| x|
File  Edit  Script  Help
if (!size(`ls -sl`)) print("nothing selected!\n");
nothing selected!
if (!size(ls("-sl"))) print("nothing selected!\n");
nothing selected!
if (!`size `ls -sl``) print("nothing selected!\n");
// Error: if (!`size `ls -sl`) print("nothing selected!\n");
//
// Error: Syntax error //
if (!`size ls("-sl")`) print("nothing selected!\n");
// Error: Invalid call to "size".  Check number and types of arguments expected by the procedure. //

if (!size(`ls -sl`)) print("nothing selected!\n");

if (!size(ls("-sl"))) print("nothing selected!\n");

if (!`size `ls -sl``) print("nothing selected!\n");

if (!`size ls("-sl")`) print("nothing selected!\n");
```

LOST & FOUND

With version 6.0 the ls command can now search over all namespaces at once. Thank Shiva and possibly Ganesha! (Maya is after all a reference from Sanskrit and not from the Central American empire.) The frustration of not finding objects that were not in the current namespace is gone by using the recursive –r flag. This flag is a toggle so add a "1" after it to activate! Here's an example with four Borg cubes in attack formation, each in a different namespace. Now you can save Federation space by identifying all of them despite their namespace cloaking!

TRACKING YOUR CUSTOMERS

If you've written any tools as procedures and would like to keep usage logs, you can use MEL to track your users. The following Unix-based code snippet for Linux only (sorry, Windows users), preferably placed near the beginning of your procedure, takes the approach of creating a file on disk each time the procedure is invoked, identifying the user in the filename.

```
string $logDirName = "/usr/home/ken/myToolLogs";
string $logFileName = getenv("USER") + system("date +%k%M%S_%Y.log");

catchQuiet(`system("touch " + $logDirName + "/" + $logFileName)`);
```

Where I'm using a directory called myToolLogs in my home directory on a Unix-based system, you would create your own directory and specify it in the $logDirName variable. After determining the directory to use, I construct the name of the log file itself by combining the user name with the time and date that the user runs the tool. The filename is also set to end with a .log extension to make it look authentic! You can create any filename you like as long as there is something unique about it so that it won't clobber another file already in the directory. The file is actually created on disk using Unix's touch command, which is executed from Maya via MEL's system command. If you're not familiar with the system command yet, you should get to know it. It's really useful, as it allows Maya to issue commands to the operating system and retrieve the results. getenv is another handy command for OS interaction and allows for retrieving the value of any environment variable, here the user's login name. To avoid annoying the user with any potential errors that may result from writing the log file (or just to play Big Brother), the system command is wrapped in the catchQuiet keyword. This keyword will allow the script to continue execution in spite of any errors that may occur and will do so hush-hush. If you plan on using the tool often yourself, you may want to exclude yourself from the logs. This can be easily accomplished by encasing the previous code in a simple if statement as follows:

```
if (getenv("USER") != "ken")
{
    string $logDirName = "/usr/home/ken/myToolLogs";
    string $logFileName = getenv("USER") + system("date
+%k%M%S_%Y.log");

    catchQuiet(`system("touch " + $logDirName + "/" + $logFileName)`);
}
```

AVOIDING GLOBAL VARIABLES WITH INTERFACE WIDGETS

Avoiding the use of global variables is often referred to as the "golden rule" of programming. It's best to stick to this as much as possible when MEL-coding as well. One area in which a lot of people resort to using global variables is interface coding. True, it's an easy way to keep track of widgets for later reference, but two techniques can help here. The first technique is to always give unique and appropriate names to widgets upon creation. The second is to capture the return value of widget creation calls, which will be the full widget path hierarchy. So, instead of writing code like this:

```
global string $unTSL = `textScrollList`;
```

write code like this:

```
string $unTSL = `textScrollList userNamesTSL`;
```

The local variable $unTSL can then be passed as a parameter to routines such as other widget callbacks like so:

```
menuItem -l "Fetch Selected Name" -c ("fetchTheName(\"" + $unTSL +
"\")");
```

Here a pop-up menu item would operate on the text scroll list via its callback fetchTheName. If the name you give the widget is indeed unique within your Maya session you can also reference the widget by name alone from another procedure as follows:

```
string $light[] = `textScrollList -q -si userNamesTSL`;
```

This will return the selected text from the scroll list widget. So, global variables bad, clever coding good! If you absolutely, positively have to use global variables it's best to give them appropriate names to avoid name clashing. This usually means long variable names as you might want to incorporate the name of your company followed by department followed by group, and so on.

LOSING WEIGHT WITH THE POUND CHARACTER

Here's a nifty trick tucked away deep in the MEL documentation that saves a lot of typing and makes interface coding more compact and logical. When defining callback routines for widgets, you often need some value from the widget to use in the callback. Instead of having to query the widget from the callback, the "#" character plus an index number can be used to retrieve the value of interest. A good example would be the use of a check box to control the enable state of another widget in an interface. Here's a code snippet that does just that:

```
window -t "Widgets & #' s" -rtf true simpleInterfaceWin;
            columnLayout mainCL;
string $ctrlCB = `checkBox -l "Enable" -v 1 ctrlCB`;
string $mainFrame = `frameLayout -lv 0 -cl 0 -cll 0 -bv 1 -bs "etchedOut"
mainFL`;
rowLayout -nc 4 -ct4 "both" "both" "both" "both";
                        button -l "Create" -al "center";
                        button -l "Add" -al "center";
                        button -l "Delete" -al "center";
                button -l "Close"  -al "center" -c "deleteUI
simpleInterfaceWin";
                        setParent ..;
                setParent ..;
checkBox -e -cc "frameLayout -e -en #1 $mainFrame" $ctrlCB;
showWindow simpleInterfaceWin;
```

A check box and frame layout are created and positioned one above the other using a column layout, and the frame layout is then populated with a few buttons. The check box's callback is then defined to toggle the enable state of a frame layout. The check box's callback is defined after the creation of the frame layout so that you can refer to the frame layout by its full widget hierarchy name, which is captured in the variable $mainFrame. Most of the other attributes used in the widget creation code are for formatting purposes only and aren't of importance here. What is important is the "#1" parameter, which will be replaced with the value of the check box. Because a check box has only one value to poll, use the number "1". Some compound widgets, such as the floatFieldGrp, can have multiple fields, which would be referenced with "#1", "#2", "#3", and so on. Execute the code to produce the window and try clicking the Enable check box on and off. You can try this trick with pop-up menus too. Cool and convenient!

ARE YOU SURE YOU WANT TO DO THAT?!

When developing MEL procedures that perform operations that are hard or impossible to undo, it's a good idea to give the user a chance to confirm the action. The command of choice for this is called confirmDialog, and it produces a pop-up window with an editable text message to the user, as well as nameable OK and Cancel buttons. All you have to do then is check the result of the command and proceed accordingly. Let's say you have an interface with a button that deletes all compiled shaders on disk (because we know how notorious RenderMan is with out-of-date shaders) and being prudent you want to give the user the chance to back out if, for instance, he or she hits the button by accident. Here's the code to do it:

```
string $confirm = `confirmDialog -title "CONFIRM"
-message ("About to delete all compiled shaders on disk! Proceed?") -button
"Delete" -button "Cancel" -defaultButton "Cancel" -cancelButton "Cancel"`;
if ($confirm == "Delete")
{
          print("deleting…");
}
```

A short and meaningful message is set for the user, and the buttons are named Delete and Cancel, appropriate for the operation being confirmed. The default button is also set to the Cancel button for safety's sake in case the user jumps the gun and hits the Enter key without thinking. We do all we can to protect the user from making costly mistakes that they'll no doubt come back to the developer to complain about. After a button is clicked, its name is returned by the confirmDialog command and is compared against the string Delete to see if the user approves of the operation. If not, move on as if nothing at all happened! At this point you may be thinking that you'd like to get some input from the user via a similar pop-up window mechanism. Think no further, MEL has got you covered with the promptDialog command. Check out the Maya documentation for its usage.

SWITCHING ON YOUR BUD, THE HUD

Remember those combat flight simulator games with the cool *Heads Up Displays* (HUDs)? Well, Maya's got them too, and you're probably already familiar with some of them, such as the camera names that appear at the bottom middle of the modeling windows and the viewing axes that appear in the bottom-left corner that you can toggle on and off from the Display, Heads Up Display submenu. The cool thing is that you can define your own HUD comprised of information that's important to you and toggle it on and off from a MEL command. The headsUpDisplay command is at the heart of the setup with which you provide the string to display, as well as the label of the string data and the area of the window in which to display the text. Here's an example that displays the full path of the current scene file in the upper middle of the modeling windows.

```
headsUpDisplay -section 2 -block 2 -blockSize "medium"
               -label "File Counts:"
    -labelFontSize "large"
               -command "file -q -sn"
               fileNameHUD;
```

The section and block parameters instruct the command where in screen space to display the HUD, and some experimentation is required as a few slots are pre-allocated to the built-in Maya HUDs and produce conflicts. The Maya docs go into a lot of detail about positioning HUDs so you'll definitely want to read through them. The label and its size are set and the command that returns the string to display is defined. Here the file command is being called directly, but you'll often want to write your own global procedure allowing you to collect and format any data you want for display. Finally a meaningful name is assigned to the HUD for future reference. To remove the HUD, you can run the following command, giving the HUD's name:

```
headsUpDisplay -remove "fileNameHUD";
```

It's also possible to keep the HUD around and toggle its visibility with the –vis parameter to the command. Heads up!

KEEPING YOUR VARIABLES HANDY

If you need to maintain variables and their values beyond the scope of a single Maya session or scene file, you can store them in the user's Maya preferences on disk via the optionVar command. Maya uses this mechanism to store such things as recent files and projects that appear in the File menu, and it comes in handy, for example, to remember user settings in proprietary MEL interfaces or to mark certain users as belonging to established groups in a project. It's a lot like cookies in the Web world. The command allows for storing scalars and arrays of type int, float, and string. You can add and delete elements from the arrays, remove variables that already exist, and list all of the current option variables in the environment. If you're writing a tool that performs a different operation for each user depending on their department, you might use the following code:

```
string $dept;
if (`optionVar -exists "userDept"`)
            $dept = `optionVar -q "userDept"`;
if ($dept == "fx")
            print("You're in the FX department!");
```

After checking to make sure that the variable exists, fetch it and then use it to determine some form of action. To create the variable initially, execute the following:

```
optionVar -stringValue "userDept" "fx";
```

SCOPING OUT THE SCRIPT EDITOR

```
M Script Editor                                          _ □ ×
File  Edit  Script  Help
string $objs = `ls -sl`;
// Error: Cannot convert data of type string[] to type string. //
string $objs[] = `ls -sl`;
// Error: string $objs[] = `ls -sl`;
 //
// Error: Invalid redeclaration of variable "$objs" as a different type. //
{
string $objs[] = `ls -sl`;
print $objs;
};
Ken_Cube
Steve_Sphere

string $objs = `ls -sl`;

string $objs[] = `ls -sl`;

{
string $objs[] = `ls -sl`;
print $objs;
}
◄ ▐                                                        ►
```

If you've done a lot of quick script development in the Script Editor window, you've no doubt encountered the "Invalid redeclaration of variable" problem. A good technique to avoid this altogether is the use of scope, in which you bracket your code snippet between curly braces ({ }). This essentially defines a block of code that is cleaned out after each execution, allowing you to change the types of the variables being created. A common mistake when declaring variables is specifying a string variable when a string array variable is required, as in the following:

```
string $objs = `ls -sl`;
Maya will complain that it can't convert data of type string[] to string.
The line needs to be changed to the following:
string $objs[] = `ls -sl`;
Maya will now complain about variable redeclaration. So, scope the code
like so:
{
string $objs[] = `ls -sl`;
}
```

Now you can merrily redeclare away. Scope up!

WHEN IN DOUBT, SEE WHAT THE NODE'S ABOUT

A great way to glean details about Maya's dependency graph nodes is by looking them up in the online documentation's *node reference* section. This has come in handy when I've expected to find an attribute related to some quality of a node but couldn't see it in any of Maya's editors. More often than not I've found what I needed in the reference, and it happened that either the attribute in question was not made keyable or was hidden from the interface. A good example is the sizing of NURBS surface normals; I couldn't find any way of setting their length in the interface. Polygon normals, on the other hand, can be displayed as long, medium, and short, but again lack custom-sizing settings via the GUI. Considering that polygon normals can at least be displayed at three different sizes, I promptly went the *node reference* and looked up the nurbsSurface node to see what it had to offer. I searched for "normal," and lo and behold, I discovered an attribute called normalsDisplayScale, or ndf for short. I tested it out in the Script Editor window, and it was exactly what I was looking for, so I built a simple GUI to let users specify length values for the selected objects' normals. I then went to the mesh node page and found an attribute called normalSize, or ns for short, that did the same for polygons. To reach the node reference, click on the "Nodes and Attributes" link located in the Developer's Resources folder at the bottom of the main documentation's left frame.

GOLLY G, WE'RE MATCHING

If not already part of it, the gmatch command should be added to your MEL toolbox. It provides a very useful way of identifying objects whose names match a specific pattern. This works great in conjunction with the ls command for performing operations on groups of objects that share a naming convention. Let's say that you're working on a car commercial, and there are a number of cars referenced in the scene file with namespaces that begin with the pattern "vehicle_####," where "####" represents an identification number. In addition, the scene contains various other namespaces for environmental geometry such as the road, a gas station, and so on. If you needed to perform some operation on the cars only, it could be easily done with the following code snippet:

```
string $ns;
for($ns in `namespaceInfo -lon`)
        if (gmatch($ns, "vehicle_????"))
                print($ns);
```

For the sake of example, we're simply printing the car's namespace but you can see how easy it is to identify the namespaces in question. The namespaceInfo command with the –lon option returns all of the namespaces in the scene, and the gmatch command sifts through them. The gmatch command accepts most common regular expression directives and returns true if it finds a match and false otherwise. gmatch is similar to using the grep command in a Unix shell.

Real World Production Methods

A.K.A. STRESS

Ah, the wild and woolly world of effects production. The saying goes that a CG artist spends half his or her life trying to get into it and the other half trying to get

Real World Production Methods

otherwise known as stress

out of it. It is definitely an acquired taste, where some have a stomach for the stress and technical challenges, and some may end up bartending or selling real estate. Either way, it is both an exhilarating and exhausting career, full of headaches and small victories along the way. To minimize the headache component, this chapter is written to provide a checklist for the final rendering phase, which is where most of the stress occurs, where the rubber meets the road and the chicken crosses it (or something like that). It can be maddening or pleasant, and I have found that these little nuggets of cheap advice save my stockpile of Excedrin from dwindling. In the end, CG production is an insatiable drive that manifests itself such that as one project fades onto the rental shelf, the ambition to pioneer CG history again renews itself. One thing we CG artists do not lack is the motivation to explore new ground.

TAMING THE RAM BEAST

RAM concerns present themselves when working with the Maya renderer, or any renderer for that matter. Maya tends to use lots of RAM, so here are some handy tricks for reducing the load. The tip in Chapter 5 entitled, "Determining Texture Resolution," should get you a long way initially. Next, under a File Texture's File Attributes, there is a check box for Use Cache. This will write textures to a hard disk cache until needed in the render, as opposed to storing everything in RAM as normal. To really take advantage of this technique, though, convert all textures to the block ordered textures (BOT) file type. Use `maya -optimizeRender original_file.mb optimized_file.mb` in a shell to automatically create BOT files for all textures in your scene. Similar to RenderMan's .tex format, it creates a proper mip-map or nesting of power of two resamples within one file, letting the renderer select the nearest one to a given screen space. This lowers RAM, speeds caching, and chooses properly screen-sized resolutions, which leads to much better anti-aliasing of textures. Also try to keep textures at a square aspect ratio at powers of two, such as 128, 256, 512, 1k, 2k, 4k, and so on. This can often fix problems such as not enough sharpness in the map or too much sharpness and resultant aliasing. The last option to reduce RAM usage is the –tw and –th Tile Height option flags in the command line renderer. You can choose a smaller tile size such as 64 that will load less geometry at a time. Lastly, one can save smaller versions of maps that you use while working to speed things up and then replace them with the hi-res version when you are doing finals.

MINIMIZING TEXTURE ALIASING

Aliasing is another of the sore spots with the Maya renderer, so these tips will help to alleviate this frustrating behavior. First, render two or three frames to check the temporal aliasing as a matter of habit; it will be impossible to see in a single frame. Using properly sized texture maps and BOT formats as discussed in the previous tip will get you pretty far to begin with. If problems persist, increase the Filter amount in the File Texture File Attributes if you have set it to less than one. Maya now defaults to Quadratic as the base filter type, which is a bit more expensive, but the expense is worth the results. Two pre- and post-filter options exist for the really tough ones. Use the Pre Filter check box below the Filter Type pull-down to soften the map before calculation. In the Render Globals, the Multi-pixel Filtering option will soften the entire image as a global solution. Use of square power of two textures as mentioned in the previous tip will help, as well as making sure the aliasing is not coming from excessive bump map settings.

 PRE AND POST MEL

Under Render Globals, Render Options there exists a handy set of functions—Pre Render MEL and Post Render MEL. As an example, this enables the application of custom render preset settings, hiding or unhiding of objects, and so on during rendering and restoring back afterward. With a bit of crafty coding, perhaps an email or a phone dialing can be set up for render completion notification.

LOCK DOWN THOSE SHADOWS

Another infuriating result from an overnight render can be unstable shadow maps, resulting in pops, slides, and artifacts. Part of the problem is native to shadow map technique, and some of it is due to Maya's implementation, but these tips will help lock them down. First, turn off Dmap Auto Focus in the shadow map attributes, adjusting the angle manually to match the cone angle. This feature attempts to optimize a shadow map's application, but it often brings in instability. Next, increase Dmap Filter Size for softer edge roping, but be careful of increases in render time. Next, use the Reuse Existing Dmaps option for static shadows. Lastly and most importantly, check that Auto Render Clip Plane is turned off in the Camera Attribute Editor and that clipping is bound to the model's extents and not exceeding the 0.1 to 20,000 ratio.

 GENERAL SPEED IMPROVEMENT

People have observed that rendering times have remained constant over the years, even as processor speeds go through the roof and RAM becomes as cheap as French fries (as a friend once noted). So, speed optimization is always welcome and relevant. In NURBS modeling, examine the models for degree 3 surfaces where degree 1 can suffice. Check revolves for excessive sections and intermediate wasted CVs. Check for manually set Advanced Tessellation over automatic settings. In poly models, look for overly high resolution meshes and pieces that can be combined. In lighting, avoid Area lights and shadow-casting Point lights. Reuse shadow maps if possible or paint them into textures. In shading, convert solid textures to 2D maps with Convert To File Texture. Lastly, use glows sparingly because these can equal the render time of geometry.

REDUCING MOTION BLUR ARTIFACTS

Motion blur problems are another fact of life in 3D rendering. Here are a few tips to help. As with any artifacting, check camera clipping first and turn off Auto Render Clip Plane as mentioned in the tip on the previous page, "Lock Down Those Shadows." If using 3D motion blur, individual object problems can be sampled higher than usual in Attribute Editor, Render Stats, Shading Samples Override. 3D motion blur has inherent problems with shadow maps, so shadows may need to be painted, or 2D motion blur may be used. With 2D motion blur, rendering with the post process of "blur2d" (described in the tip, "Motion Blur Choices," in Chapter 6, "From Home Movies to Hollywood:

Camerawork Basics") can control the output without requiring a re-render. One common artifact of 2D motion blur is a white halo surrounding objects. Make sure that your background is black and that there is no environmental fog in the scene. Another fix that can help is to set the Smooth Value to 0 in the Render Global Motion Blur attributes, or try reversing the Smooth Alpha/Color option.

   CHECK YOUR RELEASE NOTES

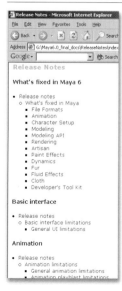

One area of the documentation many Maya artists may overlook is the Release Notes. Previously issued as separate text files, they are now integrated in the general help HTML page. The purpose of Release Notes is to state known limitations or workarounds for unique problems that other users have encountered in their work. They are generally issues that may get a bug fix in upcoming releases, or perhaps they are general limitations of the package. Either way, a workaround is offered that may or may not rectify the problem. Overall, though, they are very useful to consult during sticky problems or when a new release is made to see the potholes ahead in the road.

SETTING UP MATTES

Typically in production, separate layers are rendered, as opposed to having everything rendered in camera. The tip entitled "Layer It On" in Chapter 5 covers how to set up the basic breakdown of layers. Often, though, a compositor may request a matte render for a particular element embedded in one of these layers. Maya provides some excellent shader-centric tools for this task, located under the Matte Opacity menu in a shader's Attribute Editor. Matte Opacity is a basic control to reduce the amount of alpha contribution to the alpha channel or a render, allowing for the partial or full removal of objects in the comp. More useful, though, is the Matte Opacity Mode pull-down, giving three choices for matte behavior of an element. The default Opacity Gain allows a variable amount, as just mentioned. Solid Matte differs in that a constant value is used for the matte, overriding any partial transparency. Black Hole is very useful for knocking out full mattes because it zeroes out any matte contribution for any object behind, leaving a clean matte removal. Lastly, mattes can be created by using a black background color and a white incandescence value on the shader to achieve certain effects. With a bit of ingenuity, matte combinations can provide anything you need.

RENDER DIAGNOSTICS

Even though you may have done your render setup homework properly, Maya provides an automated check that reports some basic problems or recommendations for an optimal render. You can locate it in Render, Render Diagnostics. It reports findings in categories of Known Problems/Limitations, Warnings, and Speed/Memory Implications. It will not, however, recommend that you extract your head from the monitor, get outdoors more often, and exercise, but that would be a useful diagnostic for any Maya artist.

Z DEPTH RENDERS

Another frequently rendered layer useful in production is that of the Z depth pass. This is commonly used by compositors for a variety of functions, from establishing depth of field to desaturating over distance to atmospheric cueing. Similar to shadow map file types, a Z depth file is a non-graphic, high-bit depth indexing of depth calculations. It can be viewed as a grayscale image, however, by using Fcheck and using the "Z" key to view. Not all image file formats embed the Z channel, though, so Maya will often write it to a separate file in that case. Be sure that your compositing package can accept the format you choose because the files are always proprietary in format. Lastly, a cheap alternative to true depth maps is to use a depth shader, found online on Highend3d.com. It simply sets a grayscale range through the depth of the entire model, so that the Z depth is effectively your render. The tradeoff is that you only end up with 256 levels of depth versus the more extensive amount that resides in depth maps.

RENDERING LARGER THAN 8K

It seems there is always someone out there wondering how to create a rendering for a 5′ x 10′ poster at 300 dpi. This is generally a bad idea because higher dpi's are normally set for small print work, not billboards. However, there are occasional uses for very large renders for illustration work or fine art. Maya tops out at an 8k×8k resolution, so if more resolution is desired, here is a clever workaround. In the command-line render options, there exist flags for x and y resolution but also for sub-regions of the overall field (xLeft, xRight, yHigh, yLow). Maya only cares about the 8k limit for its current render, so by breaking up a render into smaller sub-region components, it can be assembled in a paint package to the full resolution. So, for a 10,000×5,000 pixel render, the usage command for the two would be:

```
Render -x 10000 -y 5000 -xl 0 -xr 5000 -yl 0 -yh 5000 -p first_piece
scene.mb
Render -x 10000 -y 5000 -xl 5001 -xr 10000 -yl 0 -yh 5000 -p second_piece
scene.mb
```

282 CHAPTER 10 • Real World Production Methods

A FINAL RENDER CHECKLIST

As a summary of some of the many tips in this book, here is a checklist I use frequently before an expensive overnight render at the eleventh hour of a project, along with throwing a chicken bone over my left shoulder and dancing around in circles for good luck:

- Is all geometry as optimal as possible (no wasted, flat, or excessive CVs or faces)?
- Is NURBS tessellation all set to Advanced and adjusted to screen space?
- Is camera clipping not exceeding a 0.1-to-20,000 ratio?
- Is Auto Render Clip Plane turned off in the camera attributes?
- Is bump-mapping depth set around .1 to .2 versus 1?
- Are all file texture filter values set to at least 1?
- Has a test render of two to three frames been done to check texture aliasing?
- Is Reuse Shadow Maps used for static shadows?
- Is Dmap Auto Focus turned off and set manually in spotlight shadows?
- Are all history and construction curves deleted?
- Has File, Optimize Scene Size been done?
- Has Multilister, Edit, Delete Unused been done?
- Are BOT textures used?
- Are textures sampled down to screen space and at powers of two?
- Is animation padding set to 4?
- Do you feel lucky today?

Index

Symbols

[ ] (bracket) keys, 158
(pound) character, 266
` (backtick) character, 262

: character, 84
{ } (curly braces), 270

Numbers

2D motion blur, 163, 279
3D
    developing 3D camera
        envelope, 166
    file formats for rendering, 153
    motion blur, 163, 279
    moving objects precisely in, 4
    3D stereoscopic rendering, 164

A

actions, 14
addAttr command, 250, 251
Adobe Streamline, 60
aliasing, texture, 277
aligning
    image planes, 46
    objects by snapping to second
        object, 78
    points in UV space, 83
    vertices on axis, 6
alpha channel
    extracting, 127
    premultiplication of, 137
alpha onion skins, 47
ambient lighting alternatives,
    95–96
animation. *See also*
        character animation; effects
        animation
    Animated Snapshot and
        Animated Sweep, 63
    applying custom colors to
        curves, 199
    character vs. effects, 201
    creating 3D camera
        envelope, 166

cycling curves, 183
deleting non-skin history for, 197
evaluating, 127
Flow Paths for path, 182
loading frames in tandem
    with, 160
recording mouse actions, 189
retargeting joints, 196
reverse engineering, 191
RGB lighting passes, 146
setting multiple keyframes, 186
setup for professional
    camera, 155
simplifying scenes for, 158
soft-bodied Blob-like, 220
texture maps for, 188
Animation Snapshot, 63, 77
Animation Sweep, 63
annotating objects, 5
arithmetic operators for fields, 4
arrays
    array attributes vs. attribute
        arrays, 251
    cubic point, 96
    stringArray, 251
    using, 245
arrow keys, 4
Artisan hotkeys, 174
Artisan tool, 76
aspect ratios, 153, 159
-asString flag in MEL, 260
Attach Multiple Output Meshes
    checkbox, 79
attenuation, 217
attribute arrays, 251
Attribute Editor, 30
    color mapping in, 98
    Color Remapping, 139
    comparing values for multiple
        objects, 41
    creating ramp values in, 225
    illustrated, 16
    reusing depth maps, 92
    scrubbing values in, 7
    Shadow Maps with directional
        light, 111, 116
    turbulence fields, 213, 217
    turning off shadow maps, 97
Attribute Spread Sheet
    adjusting lights via, 92

using, 8
attributes
    array attributes vs. attribute
        arrays, 251
    -asString flag, 260
    controlling in Mel, 250
    polling value of enum, 260
Auto Render Clip Plane, 157,
    278, 279
Automatic Mapping texture
    coordinate system, 81
autotracing, 60, 61

B

backgrounds
    camera projection techniques
        for, 156
    rendering, 143
backtick (`) characters, 262
Baked Simulation Index
    attribute, 236
baking light, 123
beveling edges, 73
billboards, 38
Birail command, 54
blendshapes for faces, 180
Blinn shading modes, 101
bounding boxes
    increasing refresh times with, 43
    simplifying scenes with, 158
bracket keys ([]), 158
Breakdown keys, 186
bug swarms, 214–215
Bump mapping, 49

C

caching
    particles, 221
    writing textures to hard disk
        cache, 276
camera clipping
    Auto Render Clip Plane, 157,
        278, 279
    expanding default, 13
camera pivot, 162
camera projection, 156
camerawork, 149–168
    building 3D camera
        envelope, 166